SILVER EDI

Teacher's Edition w

Interactions 1

READING

Elaine Kirn

Pamela Hartmann

Teacher's Edition by Mari Vargo

Interactions 1 Reading Teacher's Edition with Tests, Silver Edition

ISBN 13: 978-0-07-328396-8 (Teacher's Edition)
ISBN 10: 0-07-328396-7 (Teacher's Edition)
2 3 4 5 6 7 8 9 10 EUS 11 10 09 08 07

Editorial director: Erik Gundersen
Series editor: Valerie Kelemen
Developmental editor: Mary Sutton-Paul
Production manager: Juanita Thompson
Production coordinator: Vanessa Nuttry
Cover designer: Robin Locke Monda
Interior designer: Nesbitt Graphics, Inc.

Cover photo: Steve Allen/Creatas Images

www.esl-elt.mcgraw-hill.com

The **McGraw·Hill** Companies

Table of Contents

Introduction

Student Book Teaching Notes and Answer Keys

Welcome to the Teacher's Edition

The Teacher's Edition of *Interactions/Mosaic* Silver Edition provides support and flexibility to teachers using the *Interactions/Mosaic* Silver Edition 18-book academic skills series. The Teacher's Edition provides step-by-step guidance for implementing each activity in the Student Book. The Teacher's Edition also provides expansion activities with photocopiable masters of select expansion activities, identification of activities that support a Best Practice, valuable notes on content, answer keys, audioscripts, end-of-chapter tests, and placement tests. Each chapter in the Teacher's Edition begins with an overview of the content, vocabulary, and teaching goals in that chapter. Each chapter in the Student Book begins with an engaging photo and related discussion questions that strengthen the educational experience and connect students to the topic.

- **Procedural Notes**

  The procedural notes are useful for both experienced and new teachers. Experienced teachers can use the bulleted, step-by step procedural notes as a quick guide and refresher before class, while newer or substitute teachers can use the notes as a more extensive guide to assist them in the classroom. The procedural notes guide teachers through each strategy and activity; describe what materials teachers might need for an activity; and help teachers provide context for the activities.

- **Answer Keys**

  Answer keys are provided for all activities that have definite answers. For items that have multiple correct answers, various possible answers are provided. The answer key follows the procedural note for the relevant activity. Answer keys are also provided for the Chapter Tests and the Placement Tests.

- **Expansion Activities**

  A number of expansion activities with procedural notes are included in each chapter. These activities offer teachers creative ideas for reinforcing the chapter content while appealing to different learning styles. Activities include games, conversation practice, presentations, and projects. These expansion activities often allow students to practice integrated language skills, not just the skills that the student book focuses on. Some of the expansion activities include photocopiable black line masters included in the back of the book.

- **Content Notes**

  Where appropriate, content notes are included in the Teacher's Edition. These are notes that might illuminate or enhance a learning point in the activity and might help teachers answer student questions about the content. These notes are provided at the logical point of use, but teachers can decide if and when to use the information in class.

- **Chapter Tests**

  Each chapter includes a chapter test that was designed to test the vocabulary, reading, writing, grammar, and/or listening strategies taught in the chapter, depending on the language skill strand being used. Teachers can simply copy and distribute the tests, then use the answer keys found in the Teacher's Edition. The purpose of the chapter tests is not only to assess students' understanding of material covered in the chapter but also to give students an idea of how they are doing and what they need to work on. Each chapter test has four parts with items totaling 100 points. Item types include multiple choice, fill-in-the-blank, and true/false. Audioscripts are provided when used.

- **Black Line Masters (Photocopiable Masters)**

  Each chapter includes a number of expansion activities with black line masters, or master worksheets, that teachers can copy and distribute. These activities and black line masters are optional. They can help reinforce and expand on chapter material in an engaging way. Activities include games;

conversation practice; working with manipulatives such as sentence strips; projects; and presentations. Procedural notes and answer keys (when applicable) are provided in the Teacher's Edition.

- **Placement Tests**

  Each of the four language skill strands has a placement test designed to help assess in which level the student belongs. Each test has been constructed to be given in under an hour. Be sure to go over the directions and answer any questions before the test begins. Students are instructed not to ask questions once the test begins. Following each placement test, you'll find a scoring placement key that suggests the appropriate book to be used based on the number of items answered correctly. Teachers should use judgment in placing students and selecting texts.

The Interactions/Mosaic Silver Edition Program

Interactions/Mosaic Silver Edition is a fully-integrated, 18-book academic skills series. Language proficiencies are articulated from the beginning through advance levels <u>within</u> each of the four language skill strands. Chapter themes articulate <u>across</u> the four skill strands to systematically recycle content, vocabulary, and grammar.

- **Reading Strand**

  Reading skills and strategies are strategically presented and practiced through a variety of themes and reading genres in the five Reading books. Pre-reading, reading, and post-reading activities include strategies and activities that aid comprehension, build vocabulary, and prepare students for academic success. Each chapter includes at least two readings that center around the same theme, allowing students to deepen their understanding of a topic and command of vocabulary related to that topic. Readings include magazine articles, textbook passages, essays, letters, and website articles. They explore, and guide the student to explore, stimulating topics. Vocabulary is presented before each reading and is built on throughout the chapter. High-frequency words and words from the Academic Word List are focused on and pointed out with asterisks (*) in each chapter's Self-Assessment Log.

- **Listening/Speaking Strand**

  A variety of listening input, including lectures, academic discussions, and conversations help students explore stimulating topics in the five Listening/Speaking books. Activities associated with the listening input, such as pre-listening tasks, systematically guide students through strategies and critical thinking skills that help prepare them for academic achievement. In the Interactions books, the activities are coupled with instructional photos featuring a cast of engaging, multi-ethnic students participating in North American college life. Across the strand, lectures and dialogues are broken down into manageable parts giving students an opportunity to predict, identify main ideas, and effectively manage lengthy input. Questions, guided discussion activities, and structured pair and group work stimulate interest and interaction among students, often culminating in organizing their information and ideas in a graphic organizer, writing, and/or making a presentation to the class. Pronunciation is highlighted in every chapter, an aid to improving both listening comprehension and speaking fluency. Enhanced focus on vocabulary building is developed throughout and a list of target words for each chapter is provided so students can interact meaningfully with the material. Finally, Online Learning Center features MP3 files from the Student Book audio program for students to download onto portable digital audio players.

- **Writing Strand**

  Activities in each of the four Writing books are systematically structured to culminate in a *Writing Product* task. Activities build on key elements of writing from sentence development to writing single paragraphs, articles, narratives, and essays of multiple lengths and genres. Connections between writing and grammar tie the writing skill in focus with the grammar structures needed to develop each writing skill. Academic themes, activities, writing topics, vocabulary development, and critical thinking strategies prepare students for university life. Instructional photos are used to strengthen engagement and the educational experience. Explicit pre-writing questions and discussions activate prior knowledge, help organize ideas and information, and create a foundation for the writing product. Each chapter includes a self-evaluation rubric which supports the learner as he or she builds confidence and autonomy in academic writing. Finally, the Writing Articulation Chart helps teachers see the progression of writing strategies both in terms of mechanics and writing genres.

■ Grammar Strand

Questions and topical quotes in the four Grammar books, coupled with instructional photos stimulate interest, activate prior knowledge, and launch the topic of each chapter. Engaging academic topics provide context for the grammar and stimulate interest in content as well as grammar. A variety of activity types, including individual, pair, and group work, allow students to build grammar skills and use the grammar they are learning in activities that cultivate critical thinking skills. Students can refer to grammar charts to review or learn the form and function of each grammar point. These charts are numbered sequentially, formatted consistently, and indexed systematically, providing lifelong reference value for students.

■ Focus on Testing for the TOEFL® iBT

The all-new TOEFL® iBT *Focus on Testing* sections prepare students for success on the TOEFL® iBT by presenting and practicing specific strategies for each language skill area. The Focus on Testing sections are introduced in Interactions 1 and are included in all subsequent levels of the Reading, Listening/Speaking, and Writing strands. These strategies focus on what The Educational Testing Service (ETS) has identified as the target skills in each language skill area. For example, "reading for basic comprehension" (identifying the main idea, understanding pronoun reference) is a target reading skill and is presented and practiced in one or more *Focus on Testing* sections. In addition, this and other target skills are presented and practiced in chapter components outside the *Focus on Testing* sections and have special relevance to the TOEFL® iBT. For example, note-taking is an important test-taking strategy, particularly in the listening section of the TOEFL® iBT, and is included in activities within each of the Listening/Speaking books. All but two of the *Interactions/Mosaic* titles have a *Focus on Testing* section. Although *Interactions Access Reading* and *Interaction Access Listening/Speaking* don't include these sections because of their level, they do present and develop skills that will prepare students for the TOEFL® iBT.

■ Best Practices

In each chapter of this Teacher's Edition, you'll find Best Practices boxes that highlight a particular activity and show how this activity is tied to a particular Best Practice. The Interactions/Mosaic Silver Edition team of writers, editors, and teacher consultants has identified the following six interconnected Best Practices.

---

* TOEFL is a registered trademark of Educational Testing Services (ETS). This publication is not endorsed or approved by ETS.

Best Practices

Each chapter identifies at least six different activities that support six Best Practices, principles that contribute to excellent language teaching and learning. Identifying Best Practices helps teachers to see, and make explicit for students, how a particular activity will aid the learning process.

Making Use of Academic Content

Materials and tasks based on academic content and experiences give learning real purpose. Students explore real world issues, discuss academic topics, and study content-based and thematic materials.

Organizing Information

Students learn to organize thoughts and notes through a variety of graphic organizers that accommodate diverse learning and thinking styles.

Scaffolding Instruction

A scaffold is a physical structure that facilitates construction of a building. Similarly, scaffolding instruction is a tool used to facilitate language learning in the form of predictable and flexible tasks. Some examples include oral or written modeling by the teacher or students, placing information in a larger framework, and reinterpretation.

Activating Prior Knowledge

Students can better understand new spoken or written material when they connect to the content. Activating prior knowledge allows students to tap into what they already know, building on this knowledge, and stirring a curiosity for more knowledge.

Interacting with Others

Activities that promote human interaction in pair work, small group work, and whole class activities present opportunities for real world contact and real world use of language.

Cultivating Critical Thinking

Strategies for critical thinking are taught explicitly. Students learn tools that promote critical thinking skills crucial to success in the academic world.

1

Academic Life Around the World

In this chapter, students will read about college and university life for international students in higher education around the world. In the first reading, they will learn about the reasons that students choose to study abroad and why universities want international students. In the second reading, students will learn about similarities and differences in colleges and universities around the world. For example, they will learn about different systems of higher education, differences in teaching and learning methods, and the variety of facilities and services that they might find in global colleges and universities. These readings will help prepare students for the new experiences they will encounter in their academic careers.

Chapter Opener

❏ Direct students' attention to the photo and ask questions: *Who are the people in the photo?* (The photo is of Williams College students sitting in a circle outside on a lawn for class. Williams College is in Williamstown, MA.) *What are they doing? Where are they?*

❏ Put students in small groups to discuss the **Connecting to the Topic** questions.

❏ Read the quotation by John Dewey and ask students what they think it means.

❏ Put this sentence on the board: *I'm studying English because _____.* Tell students to complete the sentence with the reason they want to learn English.

❏ Put students from different language groups in pairs (if possible) to discuss the sentence.

❏ Call on students to share their ideas with the class.

❝ Education is not preparation for life; education is life itself. ❞

—John Dewey
educator, psychologist, philosopher from the U.S. (1859–1952)

Chapter Overview

Reading Skills and Strategies

Recognizing reading structure in a textbook

Recognizing main ideas

Recognizing supporting details

Recognizing topics

Getting meaning from context

Critical Thinking Skills

Synthesizing and discussing ideas from a reading

Summarizing a reading

Predicting the content of a reading

Drawing conclusions

Analyzing Internet information on higher education

Vocabulary Building

Getting meaning from context: definitions and italics

Identifying words with similar meanings

Guessing words from context

Focusing on high frequency words

Language Skills

Stating preferences and identifying reasons for
  preferences

Focus on Testing

Summarizing

Vocabulary

Nouns		Verbs	Adjectives
academic lectures	instructors	attend*	abroad*
assignments	learning resource centers	complete*	audio
atmosphere	loans*		foreign*
certificates	methods		individual
citizens*	points*		international*
developing nations	public transportation		private*
distance learning	quizzes		public*
engineering*	requirements		relaxed
exit exam	scholarships		similar
experience*	scores		
facilities	skills*		
financial aid	styles		
governments*	tuition		
immigrants	universities*		
	views*		

*These words are among the 2,000 most-frequently used words in English.

International Students

Before You Read

1 **Previewing the Topic**

- ❏ Have students look at the photos. Check comprehension by asking questions: *What do you do in a cafeteria? Who are the people in the second photo? What kind of class is it? Where do you go to study for a test?*

- ❏ Put students in small groups to practice asking and answering questions.

- ❏ Call on students to share their answers with the class.

ANSWER KEY

Answers will vary.

2 **Predicting**

Best Practice

Activating Prior Knowledge

Activities such as this allow students to tap into their prior knowledge. Students learn more effectively when new information is meaningful to them, and working in groups to discuss and think about what they already know about a topic will allow them to actively link their prior knowledge to upcoming new information.

- ❏ Put students into groups of three to discuss and write answers to the questions. Explain that it is OK to guess if they don't know the answers.

- ❏ Call on students to share their answers with the class.

- ❏ Tell students to look for the answers to the questions in the reading passage as they read.

ANSWER KEY

Answers will vary. See After You Read, Activity 7, TE page 6 for real answers.

3 **Previewing Vocabulary**

- ❏ Tell students to look at the list of vocabulary words and repeat them as you read them aloud, or listen and repeat them as you play the tape or CD.

- ❏ Have them put a check mark (✓) next to the words they know.

Read

4 **Reading an Article**

Best Practice

Making Use of Academic Content

The reading passages in this chapter introduce students to the experience of the international student, and to general lifestyles of college students around the world. These articles will enable students to better understand and navigate academic life either in their own culture or abroad.

- ❏ Have students read the article silently within a time limit (10–15 minutes), or have students follow along silently as you play the tape or CD.

- ❏ Tell them to underline any words or phrases that are new or that they don't understand.

After You Read

RECOGNIZING READING STRUCTURE IN A TEXTBOOK

- Copy the following outline on the board to show the hierarchy of the elements that make up the student book. Explain each element and ask students to look through their books for examples of each.

  Title (Interactions 1 Reading)
     Chapters
        Two readings in each chapter
           Paragraphs in each reading
              A heading for each paragraph

5 **Recognizing Reading Structure in Interactions 1 Reading**

- ❑ Tell students to use their books to find the answers to the questions. Remind them to refer to the instruction note above the activity as they work. Have them write their answers on the lines.

- ❑ Call on students to share their answers with the class.

ANSWER KEY

1. Interactions 1 Reading 2. Academic Life Around the World 3. "International Students" 4. Five 5. Conclusion and Summary

Best Practice

Scaffolding Instruction

The following series of instruction boxes and activities about topics, main ideas, and details presents new information in a step-by-step progression. This kind of scaffolded instruction allows students to thoroughly understand one part of a complex concept at a time, in this case the structure of a paragraph or article.

Strategy

Recognizing the Main Ideas

- Tell students to read the information in the Strategy box silently. When they are finished, ask volunteers to read the individual bullet points aloud.

- Explain that the main idea is the most important idea in a paragraph, and that all the other ideas in the paragraph are there to support that main idea.

- To check comprehension, tell students to look at paragraph C from the reading passage and to write down the most important idea of the paragraph.

- Call on students to share their answers. If students offer supporting details as their responses, ask them whether all the sentences in the paragraph support that one idea.

- Main idea: International students go to school abroad for different reasons.

6 **Recognizing the Main Ideas**

- ❑ Tell students to match each main idea to the paragraphs in the reading. Have them write their answers on the lines.

- ❑ Call on students to share their answers with the class.

ANSWER KEY

1. C 2. A 3. D 4. B 5. E

Recognizing Supporting Details

- Tell students to read the information in the Strategy box silently. When they are finished, ask a volunteer to read the paragraph aloud.

- To check comprehension, tell students to look again at paragraph C from the reading passage and to find one detail.

- Call on students to share their answers.

7 **Recognizing Supporting Details**

- ❏ Read the directions.

- ❏ Give students time to complete the activity as you check their work.

- ❏ Call on students to share their answers.

ANSWER KEY

1. c 2. b 3. c 4. a 5. d

- ❏ Read the directions for the second part of the activity aloud.

- ❏ Give students 5–10 minutes to complete the activity.

- ❏ Call on students to share their answers.

ANSWER KEY

Question 1: *international students*: postsecondary students from another country, *postsecondary*: after high school

Question 2: the United States (also, Canada, Great Britain, and some European countries)

Question 3: to get the experience of life in other cultures, to learn another language, to get degrees in subjects that aren't available in their countries, to learn new knowledge and skills for the government, to save money.

Question 4: for internationalism, different languages, customs, ideas, opinions, and money.

8 **Discussing the Reading**

Best Practice

Interacting with Others

Collaborative activities such as this help students get a better understanding of the ideas in the reading passage through interacting with other students. They can clarify answers and reinforce knowledge with the assistance of their group members.

- ❏ Put students into small groups to discuss answers to the questions. Ask them to take notes on their discussion.

- ❏ Call on students to share their answers with the class.

Academic Life Around the World

Before You Read

1 Previewing Vocabulary

- ❑ Tell students to look at the list of vocabulary words and repeat them after you, or listen and repeat them as you play the tape or CD.

- ❑ Have them put a check mark (✓) next to the words they know.

RECOGNIZING TOPICS, MAIN IDEAS, AND SUPPORTING DETAILS

- ◼ Tell students to read the information in the instruction note silently. When they are finished, ask volunteers to read the individual bullet points aloud.

- ◼ Explain that the topic of a paragraph is what the paragraph is about.

- ◼ To check comprehension, ask students what the main idea of a paragraph is (the most important idea).

- ◼ Ask students what a supporting detail of a paragraph is (an example or more information about the main idea).

- ◼ Tell students to look at the paragraph. Call on students to identify the topic, the main idea, and a few supporting details of the paragraph.

2 Recognizing the Topics and Main Ideas of Paragraphs

- ❑ Have students read the passage silently within a time limit (10–15 minutes), or have students follow along silently as you play the tape or CD.

- ❑ Tell them to underline any words or phrases that are new or that they don't understand.

- ❑ Tell them to do the activity when they have finished reading.

- ❑ Call on students to share their answers.

ANSWER KEY

1. University life around the world 2. A: similarities in student life in schools around the world, B: differences of education systems around the world, C: differences in teaching and learning methods and styles in schools around the world, D: facilities and services in schools around the world 3. A: In some ways, life on the campuses of institutions of higher education is the same everywhere in the world. B: Maybe student life is similar, but the system of higher education differs in countries around the world. C: Teaching and learning methods and styles differ in various cultures, at different colleges and universities, and in individual courses. D: At many institutions of higher education, resources for learning and recreation are available to students.

Read

Content Notes

- ◼ In the United States, "financial aid" is money that the government gives to college and university students to pay for school. The money is given to students who need it and can't afford to go to college without financial assistance.

- ◼ In the United States, students usually have to attend school for thirteen years before they attend a college or university. Elementary or grammar school spans kindergarten (the grade before first grade) through fifth or sixth grade. Junior high school or middle school spans sixth or seventh grade through eighth or ninth grade. High school spans ninth or tenth grade through twelfth grade. Students usually start kindergarten when they are five years old and finish high school when they are seventeen or eighteen years old.

After You Read

Strategy

Summarizing

- Tell students to read the information and the summary in the Strategy box silently. When they are finished, ask volunteers to read individual bullet points and the summary aloud.

- To check comprehension, ask volunteers to explain what a summary is, whether it's longer or shorter than the original text, and what a good summary does.

3 Summarizing a Paragraph

❑ Tell students to reread paragraph A of the previous reading. Ask volunteers to tell you, without looking at the paragraph, what the topic is, what the main idea is, and what the supporting details are. Write their responses on the board. For example:

Topic: university life in different countries

Main idea: University life is very similar all over the world.

Supporting details: Students all over the world attend classes, study, get certificates or degrees, and have interests outside of school.

❑ Ask a volunteer to tell you what the first sentence of your summary should be, using the notes you've written on the board. Ask other students to give you sentences for the second, third, and perhaps fourth sentences.

❑ As students respond, write a summary paragraph on the board. The end result should be similar to the paragraph in the Summarizing Strategy box.

❑ Put students in groups of three and read the directions to them.

❑ Have each student choose a paragraph to summarize.

❑ Have students summarize their paragraphs and read their summaries to their group members.

❑ Call on students to read their summaries to the class.

ANSWER KEY

Answers will vary.

4 Discussing the Reading

❑ Put students into small groups to discuss answers to the questions. Ask them to take notes on their discussion.

❑ Call on students to share their answers with the class.

Best Practice

Organizing Information

The following Expansion Activity will teach students to organize information using a graphic organizer. This allows students to better assimilate and recall information at a later date, a valuable study tool. In this case, students compare similarities and differences between themselves and a classmate.

REPRODUCIBLE EXPANSION ACTIVITY

- The aim of this activity is for students to get better acquainted with their classmates and to examine similarities and differences.

- Photocopy the Black Line Master **What do we have in common?** (BLM 1) and distribute to students.

- Read the directions.

- To model the activity, draw a Venn diagram on the board. Ask for a volunteer and write your name and his or her name over the two circles and "Both" over the intersecting part. Ask the student the questions in item 1 of Activity 4, page 13, and have him or her ask you the same questions. Based on his or her answers and your answers, fill in the diagram with information about the two of you.

- Have students do the same activity with a partner.

- Have volunteers copy their Venn diagrams on the board and explain them to the class.

5 Talking It Over

- ❑ Read the directions aloud.

- ❑ Tell students to complete the grid on their own. Then put students in small groups and have them share and explain reasons for their answers with their group members.

- ❑ As students work, copy the 9 squares of the grid and their headings on the board.

- ❑ When students have finished talking with their group members, go through each topic on the form, asking students to raise their hands to indicate their responses to each topic. Tally students' responses.

EXPANSION ACTIVITY

- The aim of this activity is for students to get better acquainted with their classmates and to practice interacting in English.

- Tell students to walk around the classroom and find one person who has the same answer as they do for each of the categories on the grid on page 14. Have them write their classmates' names in the appropriate boxes on the grid.

Strategy

Getting Meaning from Context: Definitions and Italics

■ Tell students to read the information and the example paragraph in the Strategy box silently. When they are finished, ask volunteers to read the individual bullet points and the paragraph aloud.

■ To check comprehension, ask volunteers to find italicized words and their definitions in the previous reading.

1 Getting Meaning from Context

❑ Read the directions aloud.

❑ Tell students to look for italics and quotation marks to find the words and phrases.

❑ Read the first example and explain if necessary. Have students complete the activity.

❑ Call on students to share their answers.

ANSWER KEY

1. an international student 2. foreign 3. abroad 4. governments 5. tuition 6. a college student from another country 7. after high school 8. countries without a high level of industrialization or technology 9. colleges and universities not supported by government money 10. legal members of a nation or country

2 Matching Vocabulary Words with Definitions

❑ Read the directions aloud and explain the first example.

❑ Have students complete the activity as you check their work.

❑ Call on students to share their answers.

❑ Read and explain the directions below the activity aloud. Tell students that they can use these techniques to study the vocabulary words.

ANSWER KEY

1. l 2. d 3. b 4. a 5. g 6. c 7. i 8. e 9. k 10. m 11. f 12. n 13. h 14. j

---

RECOGNIZING WORDS WITH THE SAME OR SIMILAR MEANINGS

■ Read and explain the information in the instruction note and explain as necessary.

3 Recognizing Words with Similar Meanings

❑ Write some simple words on the board and ask students for words that have the same or similar meanings as the words you've written (e.g., big [large, giant, huge, enormous], talk [chat, discuss, have a conversation, tell, lecture, discuss]).

❑ Read the directions aloud and explain the first example.

❑ Have students complete the activity as you check their work.

❑ Call on students to share their answers.

ANSWER KEY

1. software 2. atmosphere 3. undergraduates 4. higher 5. individual 6. a cafeteria 7. a textbook 8. titles

4 Focusing on High-Frequency Words

❑ Read the directions aloud and do the first item as a class.

❑ Have students complete the activity as you circulate and check their progress.

ANSWER KEY

1. Attend 2. experience 3. engineering
4. governments 5. skills 6. international
7. abroad 8. especially

5 **Making Connections**

❑ If you have access to a computer lab, conduct this activity in the lab so you can help students with their research. Complete the activity once as a class so students feel more comfortable doing the activity on their own. If you do not have access to a computer lab, assign this activity as homework.

❑ Have students work in pairs to share the information they found.

❑ Call on students to share their research with the class.

Best Practice

Organizing Information

Activities such as the following Expansion Activity will teach students to organize information using a graphic organizer. This allows students to better assimilate and recall information at a later date, a valuable study tool. In this case, students compare and contrast two colleges or universities.

EXPANSION ACTIVITY

■ The aim of this activity is for students to compare two colleges or universities and evaluate them to decide which of the two they prefer.

■ Photocopy the Black Line Master **Making Comparisons: Internet Search** (BLM 2) and distribute to students.

■ Read the directions.

■ Ask volunteers to list some things that they think are important when choosing a college or university to attend—facilities, class size, majors, sports teams, etc.

■ Have students complete their T-charts as they do their research.

■ Call on students to copy their T-charts on the board and explain why they prefer one school over the other.

Best Practice

Cultivating Critical Thinking

Activities such as the following summarizing activity will help students practice deductive reasoning skills. Although students may be able to identify information that is related to a given topic or appears in a reading passage, they may not have thoroughly grasped the concept of including only the most important ideas in a summary. Determining which sentences describe the most important ideas in a reading passage can help them develop this skill.

Focus on Testing   TOEFL® IBT

Summarizing

- Read and explain the information in the instruction note on summarizing.

- Point out that the summary tasks on tests are often different from what people do in academic classes.

- Go over the three points listed to help students think about and choose the sentences that best completes the summary.

Practicing Summaries

- ❏ Tell students to turn to page 8 and look again at Activity 7, Recognizing Supporting Details. Ask volunteers to explain the task in Activity 7.

- ❏ Explain that this Focus on Testing activity (Practicing Summaries) is similar to Activity 7 on page 8.

- ❏ Have students complete Focus on Testing Activity.

- ❏ Call on students to share and explain their answers.

ANSWER KEY

B, C, E

Self-Assessment Log

❑ Read the directions aloud and have students check the strategies and vocabulary they learned in the chapter.

❑ Ask volunteers to tell you where in the chapter they can find information or an activity related to each strategy.

❑ Tell students to find definitions in the chapter for any words they did not check.

EXPANSION ACTIVITY

▪ The aim of this activity is for students to internalize the definitions of the new vocabulary words.

▪ Photocopy the Black Line Master **Vocabulary Bingo** (BLM 3) and distribute to students.

▪ Read the directions. Write 20–25 vocabulary words on the board for students to choose from. You can use the vocabulary log at the end of the chapter to find the words. Complete a partial Bingo card on the board in order to model two or three examples.

▪ Model the activity by reading the definitions of two or three words. Be sure to read the definition of at least one word that is not on your card in order to show students that they don't mark anything if the word you define is not on their cards. Have students help you find the correct words on your Bingo card.

▪ Conduct the game. When a students shouts "Bingo!" check his or her answers. Optional: Give a prize to the winner.

▪ Note: Be sure to keep track of the words whose definitions you read.

2

Experiencing Nature

In this chapter, students will read about the influence of weather on our health and emotions. They will learn how certain kinds of weather can cause specific health problems like heart attacks and headaches, and how a lack of sunlight can cause depression. Students will also read about changes in our global climate. They will learn about the effects of global climate changes and the debate between scientists regarding the probable causes of these changes. These topics will encourage students to think about their environment, how they affect it, and how they are affected by it.

Chapter Opener

❑ Direct students' attention to the photo and ask questions: *What's the weather like in this photo? Where do you think this picture was taken? What time of year do you think it is? How can you tell?* (The photo is of a man and woman hiking in the Nord Fjord Region in Norway.)

❑ Put students in small groups to discuss the **Connecting to the Topic** questions.

❑ Read the quotation by Marcel Proust and ask students what they think it means.

❑ Put this sentence on the board: *I like _____ weather because _____.* Tell students to complete the sentence with the kind of weather they like and why they like it. Put students from different language groups in pairs (if possible) to discuss the sentence.

❑ Call on students to share their ideas with the class.

❝ A change in the weather is sufficient to recreate the world and ourselves. **❞**

—Marcel Proust
French novelist (1871–1922)

Chapter Overview

Reading Skills and Strategies

Identifying cause and effect

Recognizing titles and paragraph topics

Identifying main ideas

Recognizing supporting details

Critical Thinking Skills

Distinguishing between beliefs and scientific facts

Summarizing information in a paragraph

Synthesizing and discussing ideas from the reading

Building Vocabulary

Getting meaning from context from parentheses and words with similar meanings

Recognizing words with the same or similar meanings

Matching vocabulary items with examples

Language Skills

Understanding weather reports; comparing weather conditions

Stating and explaining opinions

Focus on Testing

Finding main ideas and vocabulary clusters

Vocabulary

Nouns		Verbs	Adjectives	Adverb
asthma	headaches	affects	depressed	slowly*
atmosphere	heart attacks*	increase*	extreme*	
biometeorologists	humidity	influence*	forceful*	
blizzards	hurricanes		moody	
carbon dioxide (CO_2)	meteorologists		nervous	
damage*	moods		powerful*	
desert*	pneumonia		temperature*	
disease*	rain*		typical*	
disorder	scientists*		worse*	
effects*	storms*			
floods*	strokes			
flu (influenza)	temperatures*			
	weather*			

*These words are among the 2,000 most-frequently used words in English.

The Powerful Influence of Weather

Before You Read

1 Previewing the Topic

- ❑ Have students look at the photos. Check comprehension by asking questions: *What do these pictures show? What seasons do they show?*

- ❑ Have the students read the questions on page 22 and write brief answers.

- ❑ Put students in small groups to practice asking and answering questions.

- ❑ Call on students to share their answers with the class.

ANSWER KEY

Answers will vary.

2 Predicting

> **Best Practice**
>
> **Activating Prior Knowledge**
>
> Predicting activities allow students to tap into their prior knowledge. Students learn more effectively when new information is meaningful to them, and working in groups to discuss and think about what they already know about a topic will allow them to actively link their prior knowledge to upcoming new information. In this case, students are talking about and comparing different kinds of weather.

- ❑ Put students into small groups to discuss and write answers to the questions. Explain that it is OK to guess if they don't know the answers.

- ❑ Call on students to share their answers with the class.

- ❑ Tell students to look for the answers to the questions in the reading passage as they read.

ANSWER KEY

Answers will vary.

3 Previewing Vocabulary

- ❑ Tell students to look at the list of vocabulary words and repeat them as you read them aloud, or listen and repeat them as you play the tape or CD.

- ❑ Have them put a check mark (✓) next to the words they know.

Read

> **Content Note**
>
> - ■ Doctors first identified weather-related depression in 1845, but it was officially named "Seasonal Affective Disorder" by American doctor Norman E. Rosenthal in 1984. Rosenthal felt depressed after moving from Africa to New York. He experimented with artificial light treatments and discovered that the light made him feel better.

4 Reading an Article

- ❑ Have students read the article silently within a time limit (10–15 minutes), or have students follow along silently as you play the tape or CD.

- ❑ Tell them to underline any words or phrases that are new or that they don't understand.

After You Read

Strategy

Using a Diagram to Show Cause and Effect

- To clearly organize your ideas on why things happen, you can use a diagram. Write notes on the *causes* of your topic in a column on the left side and include details on their *effects* on the right side. See the example below:

Hurricanes (Causes)	→	Dangers to People (Effects)
lots of rain in a short period of time	→	flooding, damage to homes
strong winds	→	falling trees, injuries, damage to homes, blocking roads

5 Identifying Cause and Effect

Best Practice

Organizing Information

Activities such as this will teach students to organize information from a reading passage using a graphic organizer. This allows students to better assimilate and recall information at a later date, a valuable study tool. In this case, students identify the health effects of weather mentioned in the passage.

- ❑ Tell students to read the information in the Strategy box and look back at the reading passage to find the causes and effects that complete the chart below. Have them write their answers on the lines provided in the boxes.

- ❑ Call on students to share their answers with the class.

ANSWER KEY

Types of Weather (Causes): weather, long periods of darkness

Effects on People (Effects): headaches, asthma attacks; Pneumonia

EXPANSION ACTIVITY

- The aim of this activity is for students to apply the information they've learned from the reading passage about weather.

- Bring in a weather map from a newspaper. Explain what the symbols mean. Use the vocabulary that was introduced in the reading passage.

- Have students look at the map and explain what kinds of moods or health problems the weather depicted on the map might cause, according to the reading passage.

RECOGNIZING READING STRUCTURE: TITLES AND PARAGRAPH TOPICS

- Read the information in the instruction note.

- Turn to the article "The Powerful Influence of Weather" on page 23.

- Ask a student to read the title of the article. Ask other students to read the paragraph topics.

Best Practice

Scaffolding Instruction

Activities 6, 7, and 8 are about topics, main ideas, and details. They present new information in a step-by-step progression. This kind of scaffolded instruction allows students to thoroughly understand one part of a complex concept at a time, in this case the structure of a paragraph or article.

6 **Recognizing Reading Structure: Titles and Paragraph Topics**

❑ Read the directions and explain as needed.

❑ Call on students to share their answers.

ANSWER KEY

1. f 2. b 3. e 4. a 5. g 6. d 7. c 8. h

7 **Recognizing the Main Ideas**

❑ Tell students to read each statement and decide whether or not the statement is the main idea of the paragraph indicated. Have them write *T* for true or *F* for false on the lines.

❑ Next, tell students to rewrite the false statements to make them true, based on the paragraph.

❑ Call on students to share their answers with the class.

ANSWER KEY

1. F 2. T 3. T 4. F 5. F

Possible True Sentences: 1. Biometeorologists study how weather affects our health and emotions. A definition of weather is "atmospheric conditions at a time or place." 4. The atmosphere and weather affect people's moods. People in the northern regions can feel tired and depressed, eat and sleep a lot, and work badly because of Seasonal Affective Disorder. 5. According to scientists, the cause of health problems and sad moods may be different kinds of weather.

Strategy

Recognizing Supporting Details

■ Ask a volunteer to read the paragraph aloud.

■ To check comprehension, tell students to look again at paragraph A from the reading passage and to find one detail.

❑ Call on students to share their answers.

8 **Recognizing Supporting Details**

❑ Read the directions and explain as needed.

❑ Call on students to share their answers.

ANSWER KEY

1. d 2. b 3. a 4. b 5. a

Question 1: *biometeorologists*: scientists who study how atmospheric conditions affect human health and emotions; *atmosphere*: the air around the earth; *weather*: atmospheric conditions at a time or place

Question 2: Wind can increase the number of strokes, heart attacks, headaches, and asthma attacks.

Question 3: Sudden temperature changes can increase colds, flu, pneumonia, blood diseases, and heart attacks and can lower blood pressure.

Question 4: Northern winters can make people depressed, nervous, and irritable. They can cause Seasonal Affective Disorder (SAD).

9 **Discussing the Reading**

Best Practice

Cultivating Critical Thinking

Activities such as this will help students practice challenging and analyzing assumptions rather than accepting them at face value. In this activity, students will also be able to analyze their own opinions about the usefulness of the study of the effects of weather on people, and whether or not weather affects world events.

❑ Put students into small groups to discuss answers to the questions. Ask them to take notes on their discussion.

❑ Call on students to share their answers with the class.

Global Climate Changes

Before You Read

1 Previewing Vocabulary

- ❑ Tell students to look at the list of vocabulary words and repeat them after you, or listen and repeat them as you play the audio program.

- ❑ Have them put a check mark (✓) next to the words they know.

Read

Content Notes

- ■ The name "El Niño" comes from Peruvian sailors who noticed the unusual warm current of air along the Peruvian Coast. The sailors used the name "El Niño," or "The Christ Child," because the weather condition usually happened in December.

- ■ Rainforests exist in only seven regions of the world: The Pacific northwestern region of North America, southwestern South America, the eastern Black Sea (Turkey and Georgia), the west coast of New Zealand's South Island, the west coast of Australia (Tasmania), southwestern Japan, and northwestern Europe. Most of the rainforests in Scotland, Ireland, and Iceland are gone, but there are still some rainforests left in Norway.

GETTING THE TOPIC FROM TITLES AND HEADINGS

- ■ Read the information in the instruction note and explain as needed.

- ■ Ask students to read the four paragraph headings listed.

- ■ Point out the fact that they are not complete sentences.

2 Recognizing Topics and Main Ideas

- ❑ Read the information in the instruction note on *Getting the Topic from Titles and Headings*, and explain as needed.

- ❑ Read the directions. Show students that the first paragraph is done for them.

- ❑ Have students read the passage silently within a time limit (10–15 minutes), or have students follow along silently as you play the tape or CD.

- ❑ Tell them to underline any words or phrases that are new or that they don't understand.

- ❑ Call on students to share their answers.

ANSWER KEY

A: Climate in Regions of the Globe / In different areas of the globe, the climate generally stays the same from year to year. B: General Changes in the Nature of Weather / According to some meteorologists (weather researchers), the earth's climate is changing slowly. C: Global Warming and the "El Niño" Effect / Global warming and *El Niño* are having major effects on the earth's atmosphere, weather, and climate. D: The Powerful Effect of People on Nature / Probably human beings are the main cause of the extreme effects of weather and climate changes.

3 Reading an Article

- ❑ Have students read the article silently within a time limit (10–15 minutes), or have students follow along silently as you play the tape or CD.

- ❑ Tell them to underline words or phrases that are new or that they don't understand.

After You Read

Strategy

Summarizing a Paragraph

- Tell students to read the information and the example summary in the Strategy box silently.

- To check comprehension, ask volunteers to explain the suggestions in their own words.

Best Practice

Interacting with Others

Collaborative activities such as 3, 4, and 5, which follow, help students get a better understanding of the ideas in the reading passage through interacting with other students. They can clarify answers and reinforce knowledge with the assistance of their group members.

4 Summarizing a Paragraph

- ❑ Put students in groups of three and read the directions aloud.

- ❑ Have students summarize their paragraphs and read them aloud to the other members of their groups.

- ❑ Call on students to read their summaries to the class.

ANSWER KEY

Answers will vary.

5 Discussing the Reading

- ❑ Put students into small groups to discuss answers to the questions. Ask them to take notes on their discussion.

- ❑ Call on students to share their answers with the class.

 EXPANSION ACTIVITY

- ▪ The aim of this activity is for students to think critically about the problems raised in Paragraph D of the article "Global Climate Changes" and to come up with some solutions.

- ▪ Photocopy the Black Line Master **Solutions for Global Warming** (BLM 4) and distribute to students.

- ▪ Read the directions.

- ▪ Put students in groups of three or four and have them brainstorm ideas together.

- ▪ Call on students to share their group's ideas.

6 Talking It Over

- ❑ Read the directions aloud.

- ❑ Put students into small groups. Tell them to complete the activity on their own, then share and explain reasons for their answers with their group members.

- ❑ When students have finished talking with their group members, have one member of each group share their answers and reasons with the class.

Strategy

Getting Meaning from Contexts, from Parentheses, and from Words with Similar Meanings

- Tell students to read the information and the example paragraphs in the box silently. When they are finished, ask volunteers to read individual bullet points and example paragraphs aloud.

- To check comprehension, ask volunteers to find the boldfaced words and their meanings in the previous reading.

1 Getting Meaning from Context

- Read the directions aloud.

- Read the first example and explain if necessary. Have students complete the activity.

- Call on students to share their answers.

ANSWER KEY

1. biometeorologists 2. atmosphere 3. rain, snow, humidity, air pressure 4. weather 5. strokes
6. sudden stopping of the heart 7. flu 8. lungs
9. emotional conditions and feelings 10. Seasonal Affective Disorder, long periods of darkness

2 Recognizing Words with the Same or Similar Meanings

- Read the directions aloud and explain the first example.

- Have students complete the activity as you check their work.

- Call on students to share their answers.

ANSWER KEY

1. real life 2. countries and cultures 3. condition
4. global 5. physical health 6. increase 7. science
8. common 9. air pressure 10. human beings

3 Matching Vocabulary Items with Examples

- Read the directions aloud and explain the first example.

- Have students complete the activity.

- Call on students to share their answers.

- Read and explain the directions below the activity aloud. Tell students that they can use this technique to increase their vocabulary. Model the technique with one or two examples, such as how people feel (adjectives): angry, sorry, afraid

ANSWER KEY

1. d 2. f 3. i 4. b 5. g 6. c 7. j 8. e 9. h 10. a

EXPANSION ACTIVITY

- The aim of this activity is for students to internalize the definitions of the new vocabulary words.

- Write the phrases (e.g., "atmospheric conditions") and the examples (e.g., "the ocean, seas, islands, deserts, forests") from Activity 3, page 35, on small slips of paper. Give each student either a phrase or an example.

- Have students walk around the room to find the person who has the phrase that matches their example or vice versa. For example, the student with "atmospheric conditions" would look for the student with "sun, rain, snow, wind, humidity."

4 **Focusing on High-Frequency Words**

❏ Read the directions aloud and do the first item as a class.

❏ Have students complete the activity as you circulate and check their progress.

ANSWER KEY

1. weather 2. slowly 3. typical 4. extreme
5. temperatures 6. storms 7. floods 8. rain
9. damage 10. worse

5 **Making Connections**

Best Practice

Making Use of Academic Content

Activities such as this will enable students to better understand the ideas set forth in the reading passage about the weather. The task of doing an Internet search will allow students to develop the skills they need to conduct academic research.

❏ If you have access to a computer lab, conduct this activity in the lab so you can help students with their research. Complete the activity once as a class so students feel more comfortable doing the activity on their own. If you do not have access to a computer lab, assign this activity as homework.

❏ Have students work in pairs to share the information they found.

❏ Call on students to share their research with the class.

FINDING MAIN IDEAS AND VOCABULARY CLUSTERS

- Read and explain the information in the instruction note at the top of the page.

- Have students turn to the first reading on pages 23–25. Ask them to locate the vocabulary clusters and identify the main idea of each paragraph.

Relating Vocabulary Clusters to Main Ideas

- Read the directions and have students complete this activity independently.

- Call on students to share their answers.

ANSWER KEY

1. Answers will vary. Some possibilities are *storm*, *cell*, *thunderhead*, and *those*. 2. Answers will vary. Some possibilities are *successive*, *follow* (*following*), *circulate repeatedly*, *chain of storms*. 3. The only strong possibility is *tropical storm systems*. 4. c

 EXPANSION ACTIVITY

- The aim of this activity is for students to work with the vocabulary they've encountered in this chapter. Also, have students practice doing an Internet search and making a weekly schedule.

- Photocopy the Black Line Master **Weather Forecast** (BLM 5) and distribute to students.

- Read the directions.

- Have students complete the activity as a class in the computer lab or at home.

- Have students share their weather forecasts with the class. You might have students present their information as though they were doing the weather report on the news. They could use a map drawn on the board or any other type of visual they have access to.

Self-Assessment Log

- Read the directions aloud and have students check the strategies and vocabulary they learned in the chapter.

- Ask a volunteer to tell you where in the chapter they can find information or an activity related to each strategy.

- Tell students to find definitions in the chapter for any words they did not check.

3

Living to Eat, or Eating to Live?

In this chapter, students will read about diets around the world and reasons behind the diets of particular cultures and regions. For example, they will learn how location, history, tradition, and religion affect the kinds of foods people eat. Students will also read about differing opinions on nutrition, the effects of certain kinds of food on our minds and our bodies, and the nutritional value of insects as food. These topics will encourage students to think about their own diets, how they are affected by the foods they eat, and the factors involved in their diet decisions.

Chapter Opener

❑ Direct students' attention to the photo and ask questions: *What do you see in the photo? What is the woman looking at?* (The photo is of a woman in a supermarket weighing bell peppers.)

❑ Put students in small groups to discuss the questions in the **Connecting to the Topic** questions.

❑ Read the quotation by Edmund Burke and ask students what they think it means.

❑ Put this sentence on the board: *I usually eat food that is good for me / not good for me.* Tell students to circle one choice. Put students from different language groups in pairs (if possible) to discuss the kinds of food they usually eat.

❑ Call on students to share their ideas with the class.

❝ To read without reflecting is like eating without digesting. **❞**

—Edmund Burke
British political writer (1729–1797)

Chapter Overview

Reading Skills and Strategies

Recognizing reading structure: main-idea questions for paragraph topics

Recognizing one- or two-sentence statements of the main idea

Matching paragraph titles with topics

Critical Thinking Skills

Evaluating and comparing advice and opinions about food

Summarizing paragraphs

Vocabulary Building

Getting meaning from context: italics and punctuation

Recognizing vocabulary categories

Language Skills

Making diet choices based on personal preferences and culture

Finding and following recipes

Focus on Testing

Understanding schematic tables

Vocabulary

Nouns		Verb	Adjectives	Adverb
breakfast*	fast food	diet	frozen*	probably*
bugs	fats*		universal*	
complex carbohydrates	grains*		worse*	
customs*	habits*			
dairy	insects*			
desserts	low-carb diet			
diabetes	minerals*			
diet	nutritionists			
discussion*	preferences*			
dishes*	soy products			
elements				

*These words are among the 2,000 most-frequently used words in English.

Global Diet Choices

Before You Read

1 Previewing the Topic

- ❏ Have students look at the photos. Check comprehension by asking questions: *What are some examples of fast food restaurants? What are some examples of supermarket chains?*

- ❏ Have the students read the questions on page 42 and write brief answers.

- ❏ Put students in small groups to practice asking and answering questions.

- ❏ Call on students to share their answers with the class.

2 Predicting

> **Best Practice**
>
> **Activating Prior Knowledge**
>
> Activities such as predicting allow students to tap into their prior knowledge. Students learn more effectively when new information is meaningful to them, and working in groups to discuss and think about what they already know about a topic will allow them to actively link their prior knowledge to upcoming new information. In this case, students are talking about different types of diets and fast food.

- ❏ Put students into small groups to discuss and write answers to the questions. Explain that it is OK to guess if they don't know the answers.

- ❏ Call on students to share their answers with the class.

- ❏ Tell students to look for the answers to the questions in the reading passage as they read.

ANSWER KEY

Answers will vary.

3 Previewing Vocabulary

- ❏ Tell students to look at the list of vocabulary words and repeat them after you or listen and repeat them as you play the tape or CD.

- ❏ Have them put a check mark (✓) next to the words they know.

Read

4 Reading an Article

- ❏ Have students read the passage silently within a time limit (10-15 minutes), or have students follow along silently as you play the tape or CD.

- ❏ Tell them to underline any words or phrases that are new or that they don't understand.

After You Read

> **Best Practice**
>
> **Scaffolding Instruction**
>
> The following series of instruction boxes and activities about main ideas and supporting details presents new information in a step-by-step progression. This kind of scaffolded instruction allows students to thoroughly understand one part of a complex concept at a time, in this case the structure of a paragraph or article.

5 Recognizing Reading Structure

- ❏ Read the information in the *Recognizing Reading Structure* instruction note and explain as needed.

- ❏ Read the directions for this activity and do the first item as a class if necessary.

- ❏ Have students complete the activity.

- ❏ Call on students to share their answers with the class.

ANSWER KEY

1. E   2. C   3. D   4. B   5. A

 EXPANSION ACTIVITY

- ■ The aim of this activity is for students to relate their own lives to the reading passage by observing and analyzing their own eating habits.

Directions:

- ■ Photocopy the Black Line Master **A Food Diary** (BLM 6) and distribute to students.

- ■ Read the directions.

- ■ At the end of the five-day period, have students share their food diaries and observations with the class. An example of an observation is "I ate a lot of pasta, but I didn't eat much fruit."

RECOGNIZING ONE- OR TWO-SENTENCE STATEMENTS OF THE MAIN IDEA

- ■ Read the information in the instruction note.

- ■ Remind students that the main idea is the most important idea in a paragraph, and that all the other ideas in the paragraph are there to support that main idea.

- ■ To check comprehension, ask a volunteer to identify the main idea of Paragraph A.

6 Recognizing One- or Two-Sentence Statements of the Main Idea

- ❑ Tell students to compare each statement to a paragraph in the reading and decide whether or not the statement is the main idea of the paragraph. Have them write *T* for true or *F* for false on the lines.

- ❑ Call on students to share their answers with the class.

- ❑ Next, tell students to rewrite the false statements to make them true, based on the paragraphs.

- ❑ Call on students to share their answers with the class.

- ❑ Finally, have students look at how the true sentences answer the questions in Activity 2, page 43.

ANSWER KEY

1. T   2. F   3. F   4. F   5. F

Possible new sentences: 2. There's a lot of variety in fast food around the world. Each country has its own kinds of fast food. But the atmosphere of fast food chains is similar around the world. 3. Individual diet decisions are often based on habits, convenience, cost, and beliefs about health and beauty. 4. The diets of whole cultures and regions come from location, history, tradition, and religion. 5. Universally, more and more meals include basic necessary food elements—protein, carbohydrates, and fats. Only a few families grow their own food. Most buy food from eating places and markets.

7 Recognizing Supporting Details

- ❑ Read the directions.

- ❑ Give students a time limit (10–15 minutes) to complete the activity.

- ❑ Tell students they can go back to Activity 2 on page 43 to check their answers.

- ❑ Call on students to share their answers.

ANSWER KEY

Unrelated sentences:

1. a   2. c   3. d   4. b   5. d

8 Discussing the Reading

> **Best Practice**
>
> **Cultivating Critical Thinking**
> Activities such as this will help students practice expressing their own opinions and analyzing their reasons for doing certain things. In this activity, students will share opinions about fast food restaurants and analyze their individual diet choices.

- ❑ Put students into small groups to discuss answers to the questions.

- ❑ Ask them to take notes on their discussions.

- ❑ Call on students to share their answers with the class.

Facts About Food

Before You Read

1   **Previewing Vocabulary**

- ❑ Tell students to look at the list of vocabulary words and repeat them after you or listen and repeat them as you play the audio program.

- ❑ Have them put a check mark (✓) next to the words they know.

Read

2   **Matching Paragraph Titles with Topics**

- ❑ Read the information in the instruction note and explain as needed.

- ❑ Read the directions. Show students that the first topic is done for them.

- ❑ Have students complete the activity and share their answers.

ANSWER KEY

1. d   2. a   3. c   4. b

3   **Choosing Titles and Recognizing Topic Sentences**

- ❑ Read the directions. Show students that the first paragraph is done for them.

- ❑ Have students read the passage silently within a time limit (10–15 minutes) or have students follow along silently as you play the tape or CD.

- ❑ Tell them to underline any words or phrases that are new or that they don't understand.

- ❑ Call on students to share their answers.

ANSWER KEY

Possible answers:

A: Food Fights—Everywhere on earth there are "food specialists" with opposite (or different) opinions on the best kinds of nutrition for various purposes. B: Food for Thought—Various ingredients and dishes affect the mind in different ways, and some kinds of nourishment have better effects on the brain than others. C: Getting the Bugs Out—For several reasons, insects are an important kind of food in the global diet, and they may become a more common ingredient in the future. D: The Fat of the Land—The growing similarities in diet and eating habits around the world are influencing people of various cultures in different ways.

After You Read

Strategy

More About Summarizing

- ■ Tell students to read the information and the sample summary in the Strategy box silently.

- ■ To check comprehension, ask volunteers to explain the suggestions in their own words.

4   **Summarizing**

- ❑ Put students in groups of three and read the directions aloud. Have each student choose one paragraph to summarize.

- ❑ Have students summarize their paragraphs and read their summaries to their group members.

- ❑ Call on students to read their summaries to the class.

ANSWER KEY

Answers will vary.

5 Discussing the Reading

Best Practice

Interacting with Others

Collaborative activities such as this help students get a better understanding of the ideas in the reading passage through interacting with other students. This activity provides students with opportunities to clarify answers and reinforce knowledge with the assistance of their group members.

- ❑ Read the directions aloud and explain if necessary.

- ❑ Put students into groups of four to discuss answers to the questions. Tell students to take notes during their discussions.

- ❑ Call on students to share their answers with the class.

EXPANSION ACTIVITY

- ■ The aim of this activity is for students to practice using food vocabulary.

- ■ Explain the rules of Twenty Questions: One person thinks of something and the rest of the class asks no more than 20 Yes/No questions to try to guess what the person is thinking of. For example, a person thinks of an animal and the class asks questions like "Is it big?" "Does it have fur?" They can guess what the answer is at any time.

- ■ Before you begin to play, list some food-related adjectives on the board (e.g. spicy, salty, sweet, sour) and review them with the class.

- ■ Tell the class you are thinking of a kind of food. Play the game.

- ■ Allow students to take turns thinking of a food and having the class ask questions.

6 Talking It Over

- ❑ Read the directions aloud.

- ❑ Put students into small groups. Tell them to complete the activity on their own, then share and explain reasons for their answers with their group members.

- ❑ When students have finished talking with their group members, have them share their answers and reasons with the class.

ANSWER KEY

1. O 2. O 3. O 4. F* 5. F* 6. F* 7. O 8. F* 9. O 10. O

(*Note: The answers to some of these questions may change due to new research findings.)

Strategy

Getting Meaning from Context: Italics and Punctuation Clues

- Tell students to read the information in the Strategy box silently. When they are finished, ask volunteers to read individual bullet points and the paragraph aloud.

- To check comprehension, ask volunteers to find italicized words and their meanings in the previous reading.

1 Getting Meaning from Context: Italics and Punctuation Clues

❏ Read the directions aloud.

❏ Read the first example and explain if necessary.

❏ Have students complete the activity.

❏ Call on students to share their answers.

ANSWER KEY

1. diet 2. diet 3. fast food 4. universal 5. tacos and burritos 6. diabetes 7. low-carb diet 8. complex carbohydrates 9. soy products 10. dairy

Strategy

Recognizing Vocabulary Categories

- Tell students to read the information in the Strategy box silently. When they are finished, ask volunteers to read individual bullet points and the paragraph aloud.

- To check comprehension, write two category headings—*Animals, People*—on the board. Then write a list of nouns on the board: teacher, cat, horse, doctor, student, neighbor.

- Ask students to tell you which category each word belongs in. As they reply, write their answers under the appropriate categories.

2 Recognizing Vocabulary Categories

Best Practice

Organizing Information

Activities such as this will teach students to organize information from a reading passage using a graphic organizer. This allows students to better assimilate and recall information at a later date, a valuable study tool. In this case, students categorize vocabulary words.

❏ Read the directions aloud and explain the four examples.

❏ Have students complete the activity as you check their work.

❏ Call on students to share their answers.

ANSWER KEY

People: college students, citizens, classmates, instructors, meteorologists, graduates, nutritionists, immigrants, foreign students, teachers, professors, language learners, specialists, scientists, international students, researchers, doctors

Places: school, a college campus, restaurants, the whole world, the desert, Colombia, South America, a classroom, swimming pools, mountain areas, a tropical rain forest, Vietnam and Thailand, The Czech Republic, a university, European countries, southern Africa, developing nations, tennis courts, snack bars, continents

Possible Foods: beef and pork, pork or bacon, bugs, hamburgers, sandwiches, sushi and tempura, insects, dairy products, candy and cookies, salads, vegetables, fruit, grains and breads, soy products, home-cooked, shellfish, tiramisu, ice cream, rice and pasta, desserts, chicken and poultry

Human Conditions: sickness or illness, sadness, moody, perfect health, heart disease, asthma, diabetes, headaches, high blood pressure, hunger, physical beauty, flu or pneumonia, emotions, a stroke, cancer

3   Practicing with Categories

- ❏ Read the directions aloud and explain the first example.

- ❏ Have students complete the activity as you check their work.

- ❏ Call on students to share their answers.

- ❏ Read and explain the directions at the end of the activity aloud. Tell students that they can use this technique to increase their vocabulary.

ANSWER KEY

1. d 2. g 3. h 4. c 5. b 6. e 7. f 8. j 9. a 10. i

EXPANSION ACTIVITY

- ■ The aim of this activity is for students to practice vocabulary words and to internalize the concept of categories.

- ■ Explain that you will name a category, and students will have one minute to write down as many words in that category as they can think of. Possible categories: people, places, foods, human conditions, countries, weather conditions, vegetables, beverages, subjects of college study.

- ■ When the minute is up, ask how many students wrote five things, ten things, etc., in order to find out who wrote down the most things.

- ■ Play as many times as you like.

4   Focusing on High-Frequency Words

- ❏ Read the directions aloud and do the first item as a class.

- ❏ Have students complete the activity as you circulate and check their progress.

ANSWER KEY

1. fats 2. breakfast 3. grains 4. dishes
5. minerals 6. frozen 7. probably 8. customs
9. preferences 10. worse 11. discussion

5   Making Connections

Best Practice

Making Use of Academic Content

Research activities such as this will enable students to better understand the ideas set forth in the reading passage. The task of doing an Internet search will also allow students to develop the skills they need to conduct academic research.

- ❏ If you have access to a computer lab, conduct this activity in the lab so you can help students with their research. Complete the activity once as a class so students feel more comfortable doing the activity on their own. If you do not have access to a computer lab, assign this activity as homework.

- ❏ Have students work in pairs to share the information they found.

- ❏ Call on students to share their research with the class.

UNDERSTANDING SCHEMATIC TABLES

- Read the information in the instruction note and explain as necessary.

- Read the directions and have students complete the activity.

- Call on students to share their answers.

ANSWER KEY

Personal reasons for choosing a diet item: A, D, G

Cultural reasons for choosing a diet item: C, F, H

EXPANSION ACTIVITY

- The aim of this activity is for students to find out more about the subject of the reading passages in this chapter and to practice doing research.

- Photocopy the Black Line Master **Finding Food Facts** (BLM 7) and distribute to students.

- Read the directions.

- Have students complete the activity in the computer lab or on their own as homework.

- Have students share their findings with the class.

Self-Assessment Log

- ❑ Read the directions aloud and have students check the strategies and vocabulary they learned in the chapter.

- ❑ Ask a volunteer to tell you where in the chapter they can find information or an activity related to each strategy.

- ❑ Tell students to find definitions in the chapter for any words they did not check.

In the Community

In this chapter, students will read about the various ways that people usually give directions in different parts of the world. For example, they will learn that in some places, people use landmarks in their directions while in others, people use distances or street names. Students will also read about laws around the world, some of them very practical and some of them quite unusual. These topics will encourage students to consider the purposes, effects, and practicality of the laws in their own communities.

Chapter Opener

❑ Direct students' attention to the photo and ask questions: *What is happening in the picture? Are street musicians common in your country?* (This photo is of students from Moscow playing ethnic music in front of a church in New York City.)

❑ Put students in groups and have them discuss the questions in the **Connecting to the Topic** section.

❑ Read the quotation by Saint Augustine of Hippo and ask students what they think it means.

❑ Put this sentence on the board: *I like / don't like to travel because* _____. Tell students to circle one choice (*like* or *don't like*) and complete the sentence. Put students from different language groups in pairs (if possible) to discuss their sentences.

❑ Call on students to share their ideas with the class.

❝ The world is a book, and those who do not travel read only a page. ❞

—Saint Augustine of Hippo
philosopher and Catholic theologian (354–430)

Chapter Overview

Reading Skills and Strategies

Identifying paragraph and whole reading topics

Identifying main ideas by asking questions

Using punctuation to recognize supporting details

Skimming for topics and main ideas

Critical Thinking Skills

Understanding and giving directions

Paraphrasing information

Vocabulary Building

Getting the meaning from context: finding illustrations of words

Recognizing words with similar meanings and meaning categories

Recognizing nouns and verbs

Finding definitions of vocabulary items

Language Skills

Comparing and contrasting, and evaluating different laws

Focus on Testing

Answering negative fact questions

Vocabulary

Nouns		Verbs	Adjectives	Adverbs
body language	murder*	buy*	illegal	rarely*
directions*	pedestrians	gesture	serious*	seldom*
distances*	procedures	measure*	strange*	
expressions*	residents	motion*		
fine*	restaurants*	smoke*		
flights*	robbery	turn*		
gestures	smoking*			
health*	teenagers			
landmarks	travelers			
laws*	turn			
lot*	vehicles			
movements*	wine*			

*These words are among the 2,000 most-frequently used words in English.

How Can I Get to the Post Office?

Before You Read

1   Previewing the Topic

- ❑ Have students look at the illustration.

- ❑ Have the students read the questions on page 62 and write brief answers.

- ❑ Put students in small groups to practice asking and answering questions.

- ❑ Call on students to share their answers with the class.

2   Predicting

> **Best Practice**
>
> **Activating Prior Knowledge**
>
> Activities such as predicting allow students to tap into prior knowledge. Students learn more effectively when new information is meaningful to them, and working in groups to discuss and think about what they already know about a topic will allow students to actively link their prior knowledge to upcoming new information. In this case, students are discussing their experiences of asking for and giving directions.

- ❑ Put students into small groups to discuss and write answers to the questions. Explain that it is OK to guess if they don't know the answers.

- ❑ Call on students to share their answers with the class.

- ❑ Tell students to look for the answers to the questions as they read "How Can I get to the Post Office?"

ANSWER KEY

Answers will vary.

3   Previewing Vocabulary

- ❑ Tell students to look at the list of vocabulary words and repeat them after you, or listen and repeat them as you play the audio program.

- ❑ Have them put a check mark (✓) next to the words they know.

Read

4   Reading an Article

- ❑ Have students read the passage silently within a time limit (10–15 minutes), or have students follow along silently as you play the tape or CD.

- ❑ Tell them to underline any words or phrases that are new or that they don't understand.

After You Read

> **Best Practice**
>
> **Scaffolding Instruction**
>
> The following series of instruction boxes and activities about identifying main ideas and topics presents new information in a step-by-step progression. This kind of scaffolded instruction allows students to understand one part of a complex concept at a time, in this case the structure of a paragraph or article.

IDENTIFYING PARAGRAPH AND WHOLE READING TOPICS

- ▪ Read the information in the instruction note Identifying Paragraph and Whole Reading Topics.

- ▪ Go over the structure diagram.

5 **Identifying Topics of Paragraphs**

❑ Read the directions for the activity and explain as needed.

❑ Have students complete the activity.

❑ Call on students to share their answers with the class.

ANSWER KEY

A. Introduction to the reading B. Directions in Japan C. Directions in the United States D. Directions on the Internet E. Directions in Los Angeles F. Directions in Greece G. Directions in the Yucatan H. Conclusion, Body language

Subject: b

EXPANSION ACTIVITY

■ The aim of this activity is for students to practice asking for and giving directions.

■ Photocopy the Black Line Master **Asking for and Giving Directions** (BLM 8) and distribute to students.

■ Read the directions.

■ Review language for giving directions (turn right on X Street/at the X, turn left on X Street/at the X, go straight for X blocks).

■ Have students complete the activity.

■ When students have completed writing their directions, have them work with partners to take turns asking for and giving directions. Pair students who have written directions to different places.

Strategy

Identifying the Main Idea by Asking Questions

■ Read the information in the Strategy box and explain as needed.

■ Remind students that the main idea is the most important idea in a paragraph, and that all the other ideas in the paragraph are there to support that main idea.

■ To check comprehension, ask a volunteer to ask and answer a question about Paragraph A.

6 **Identifying the Main Idea by Asking Questions**

❑ Tell students to match each incomplete question to a paragraph in the reading and then complete it.

❑ Call on students to share their answers with the class.

ANSWER KEY

1. What is 2. How do people give 3. How do people give 4. What are 5. How do people give 6. How do people give 7. How do people give 8. What is 9. people give

7 **Changing False Statements to True Statements**

❑ Read the directions and do the first item as a class.

❑ Give students time to complete the activity. Then call on students to share their answers with the class.

ANSWER KEY

Possible new sentences:

1. If you don't carry a map on your travels, you have to ask for directions. 2. In Japan, people use landmarks in their directions because most streets don't have names. 3. In the American Midwest, people will use directions like north, south, east, and west and distances when they give you directions because there aren't many landmarks. 4. Many people around the world can get street directions on the Internet. 5. In Los Angeles, the most common way to give directions is in time. 6. In Greece, people usually gesture or say, "Follow me," because most visitors don't speak Greek. 7. In Yucatan, Mexico, people will usually give you an answer even if they don't know how to get somewhere because they think it's impolite to just say "I don't know." 8. All over the world, you may not understand a person's language, but you can probably understand their body language. 9. In various cultures around the world, people give directions to travelers and tourists in different ways.

Strategy

Using Punctuation to Recognize Supporting Details

■ Have students read the information in the Strategy box silently.

■ Read the first example aloud. Write this example on the board without punctuation:

> *There are a lot of countries I want to visit Japan Korea and Mexico.*
>
> *(Answer: There are a lot of countries I want to visit—Japan, Korea, and Mexico.)*

■ Ask students to tell you where the colon (**:**) and the commas (**,**) belong in that sentence.

■ Read the second example aloud. Write this example on the board without punctuation:

> *I go to Tokyo every summer my grandmother lives there.*
>
> *(Answer: I go to Tokyo every summer; my grandmother lives there.)*

■ Ask students to tell you where the semicolon belongs in that sentence.

■ Read the third example aloud. Write this example on the board without punctuation:

> *The tourist asked me, How can I get to the post office?*
>
> *(Answer: The tourist asked me, "How can I get to the post office?")*

■ Ask students to tell you where the quotation marks belong in that sentence.

8 **Using Punctuation to Recognize Supporting Details**

❏ Read the directions aloud and do the first item as a class.

❏ Have students complete the activity.

❏ Call on students to share their answers with the class.

ANSWER KEY

Possible answers:

1. Never carry a map. 2. You can have a good time, practice a new language, meet new people, and learn new customs. 3. Most streets don't have names. 4. One example of Japanese directions is "Go straight down to the corner. Turn left at the big hotel with the sushi bar and go past the fruit market. The post office is across from the bus stop—next to the fast-food fried chicken place." 5. Some examples of directions from residents of the American Midwest are "Take this road here. Go straight north for two miles," or, "Keep to the left around the curve. Then merge with Local Route 12." 6. Some examples of street directions from websites are

"Take I-40 26 miles," or, "At Exit 5B, take Ramp (RIGHT) towards Oklahoma City, Oklahoma."
7. People in Los Angeles don't give directions in distance because they almost always drive, so they don't know how far things are. 8. Greeks seldom give directions in words because most tourists don't speak Greek. 9. If a resident of New York City doesn't know how to get somewhere, he or she might say, "Sorry, I have no idea" and walk away quickly. 10. A resident of Yucatan won't answer, "I don't know," to a lost tourist because he or she might think it's impolite. 11. A person might give directions with body language by pointing in a particular direction.

Activity 2 Questions, Possible answers:

1. Answers will vary. 2. Some examples of street directions from websites are, "Take I-40 26 miles," or, "At Exit 5B, take Ramp (RIGHT) towards Oklahoma City, Oklahoma." 3. If a person doesn't know how to get somewhere, he or she can say "I don't know." 4. Body language can help you get around a community because many gestures, like pointing, are the same all over the world.

9 Discussing the Reading

Best Practice

Interacting with Others

These types of collaborative activities help students get a better understanding of the ideas in the reading passage through interacting with other students. They can clarify answers and reinforce knowledge with the assistance of their group members.

❑ Put students into small groups to discuss answers to the questions. Ask them to take notes on their discussion.

❑ Call on students to share their answers with the class.

REPRODUCIBLE EXPANSION ACTIVITY

■ The aim of this activity is for students to further explore the concept introduced in the reading passage.

■ Photocopy the Black Line Master **Real or Not Real?** (BLM 9) and distribute to students.

■ Read the directions.

■ Have students complete the activity and share their answers.

ANSWER KEY

1. R 2. R 3. NR 4. NR 5. R 6. R 7. NR 8. R 9. R 10. R

The Laws of Communities

Before You Read

1 Previewing Vocabulary

❑ Tell students to look at the list of vocabulary words and repeat them after you, or listen and repeat them as you play the tape or CD.

❑ Have them put a check mark (✓) next to the words they know.

Read

Strategy

Skimming for Topics and Main Ideas

■ Read the information in the Strategy box and explain as needed.

■ To check comprehension, ask students to explain how skimming is a useful tool.

2 Skimming for Topics

❑ Read the directions and do the first item as a class.

❑ Have students complete the activity and share their answers.

ANSWER KEY

D, B, C, A

3 Skimming for Main Ideas

❑ Read the directions.

❑ Have students read the passage silently within a time limit (10–15 minutes), or have students follow along silently as you play the tape or CD.

❑ Tell them to underline any words or phrases that are new or that they don't understand.

❑ Call on students to share their answers.

ANSWER KEY

A. C B. A C. B D. A

After You Read

Strategy

Learning to Paraphrase

■ Tell students to read the information and the examples in the Strategy box silently.

■ To check comprehension, ask questions: *What is a paraphrase? What is the first thing you must do when you paraphrase? What else do you do when you paraphrase?*

■ Ask students to reread paragraph B from the article "How Can I Get to the Post Office?" on pages 63–65.

■ Ask them to tell you what the main idea of the paragraph is without reading out of the paragraph. Write their response on the board.

■ Ask students to tell you in their own words what the other ideas in the paragraph are.

■ Write their responses on the board, and have the class help you put the ideas together to form a paraphrased summary of the original paragraph.

4 Paraphrasing

❑ Put students in groups of three and read the directions aloud.

❑ Have students summarize their paragraphs and read their summaries to their group members.

❑ Call on students to read their summaries to the class.

ANSWER KEY

Answers will vary.

5 Discussing the Reading

> **Best Practice**
>
> **Interacting with Others**
> These types of collaborative activities help students get a better understanding of the ideas in the reading passage through interacting with other students. They can clarify answers and reinforce knowledge with the assistance of their group members.

- ❏ Read the directions aloud and explain if necessary.
- ❏ Put students into groups of four to discuss their answers to the questions.
- ❏ Call on students to share their answers with the class.

6 Talking It Over

- ❏ Read the directions aloud.
- ❏ Put students into small groups. Tell them to complete the activity on their own, then share and explain reasons for their answers with their group members.
- ❏ When students have finished talking with their groups, have them share their answers and reasons with the class.

ANSWER KEY

Answers will vary.

Strategy

Getting Meaning from Context: Finding Illustrations of Words

■ Have students read the information in the Strategy box silently.

■ To check comprehension, write these sentences on the board and ask students to identify the categories and their illustrations:

> Some countries have a lot of rules about legal and illegal individual activities. For instance, in most places in the United States, no one under 21 can buy or drink alcohol legally. (category: illegal individual activities; illustration: no one under 21 can...)

> In every country and culture of the world, there are laws against serious offenses, such as murder, robbery, violence against people, and the like. (category: serious offenses; illustrations: murder, robbery, violence against people)

1 Finding Illustrations of Words

❑ Read the directions aloud.

❑ Read the first example and explain if necessary. Have students complete the activity.

❑ Call on students to share their answers.

❑ Read and explain the directions below the activity aloud. If time allows, have students complete this part of the activity in small groups.

ANSWER KEY

Answers will vary. Possible answers:

1. big hotel, sushi bar, fruit market, bus stop, fast-food fried chicken place 2. take this road here, make a right turn, keep to the left around the curve, merge with Local Route 12, turn left at Main Street, go to the third streetlight and turn

right, take the I-40 26 miles, go straight (east), enter Texas, keep left (Northwest) 8.7 miles; turn right, merge onto Turner Turnpike; at Exit 5B, take Ramp (RIGHT) towards Oklahoma City, Oklahoma 3. go straight north for two miles, go another mile in a northeast direction, go straight for five blocks, the post office is two blocks up on your left, take the I-40 26 miles, keep left (Northwest) 8.7 miles 4. facial expressions, gestures, movements, point

Strategy

Recognizing Words with Similar Meanings and Meaning Categories

■ Tell students to read the information in the instruction note silently. When they are finished, ask volunteers to read individual bullet points and the paragraph aloud.

■ To check comprehension, write two lists of words on the board:

> tourist, visitor, traveler
>
> China, Egypt, Vietnam, Korea

■ Ask students how these words belong together. Do they have similar meanings or are they in the same category? (List 1: similar meanings, List 2: same category)

2 Identifying Similar Meanings and Meaning Categories

❑ Read the directions aloud and explain the two examples.

❑ Have students complete the activity as you check their work.

❑ Call on students to share their answers.

❑ Read and explain the directions below the activity aloud. Tell students that they can use this technique to increase their vocabulary.

ANSWER KEY

1. C (types of transportation) 2. S 3. C (cities)
4. S 5. S 6. C (street and road signs) 7. C
(directions) 8. S 9. C (punctuation) 10. S

Strategy

Recognizing Nouns and Verbs

■ Read the information in the box.

■ To check comprehension, write these
sentences on the board with words
underlined as shown. Ask students to tell
whether the underlined words are nouns or
verbs:

Can I <u>discuss</u> something with you? (verb)

Can we have a <u>discussion</u>? (noun)

I'll <u>walk</u> to school tomorrow. (verb)

I think I'll take a <u>walk</u> this afternoon. (noun)

3 Recognizing Nouns and Verbs

❏ Read the directions aloud and explain the first
example.

❏ Have students complete the activity as you
check their work.

❏ Call on students to share their answers.

❏ Read and explain the directions below the
activity aloud. Tell students that they can use
this technique to increase their vocabulary.

ANSWER KEY

1. travelers 2. prefer 3. directions 4. turn
5. residents 6. measure 7. motions, gestures
8. expressions, movements 9. murder, robbery
10. smoke, drink

■ The aim of this activity is for students to
practice vocabulary words and to internalize
the concept of similar meanings and
categories.

■ Explain that you will say a word followed
by either "category" or "similar meaning."
Students will have thirty seconds to write
down as many words as they can either in the
same category as the word you say, or with a
similar meaning to the word you say. Possible
category words: tea (beverages), student
(people), United States (countries), hurricane
(weather conditions), South America
(continents), train (transportation). Possible
"similar meaning" words: illegal, gesture,
pedestrian, teacher, school, tourist.

■ After each word, ask how many students
wrote five things, ten things, etc., in order to
find out who wrote down the most things.
Have students share the words they wrote
down.

■ Play as many times as you like.

4 Finding Definitions of Vocabulary Items

❏ Read the directions aloud and explain the first
example.

❏ Have students complete the activity as you
check their work.

❏ Call on students to share their answers.

ANSWER KEY

1. d 2. h 3. f 4. a 5. j 6. b 7. g 8. c 9. e 10. i

5 Focusing on High-Frequency Words

❏ Read the directions aloud and do the first item
as a class.

❑ Have students complete the activity on their own as you circulate and check their progress.

❑ Go over the answers.

ANSWER KEY

1. customs 2. lot 3. smoking 4. buy 5. wine
6. law 7. public 8. restaurants 9. habits
10. health

6 Making Connections

Best Practice

Making Use of Academic Content

Activities such as this will enable students to better understand the ideas set forth in the reading passage about laws. The task of doing an Internet search will allow students to develop the skills they need to conduct academic research.

❑ If you have access to a computer lab, conduct this activity in the lab so you can help students with their research. Complete the activity once as a class so students feel more comfortable doing the activity on their own. If you do not have access to a computer lab, assign this activity as homework.

❑ Have students work in pairs to share the information they found.

❑ Call on students to share their research with the class.

TOEFL® iBT

ANSWERING NEGATIVE QUESTIONS ON TESTS

- Read the information in the instruction note on Answering Negative Questions on Tests and explain as needed.

- Read the directions and have students complete the activity.

- Call on students to share their answers.

ANSWER KEY

1. B 2. A 3. C

Best Practice

Cultivating Critical Thinking

Activities such as the following expansion activity will help students practice expressing their own opinions and analyzing their reasons for doing certain things. In this activity, students will share ideas for new laws for their school. Then they consider why these new laws might be useful, and analyze whether or not the same laws would be good for their homes.

 EXPANSION ACTIVITY

- The aim of this activity is for students to further explore the concepts introduced in the reading passages.

- Photocopy the Black Line Master **Making New Laws** (BLM 10) and distribute to students.

- Read the directions.

- Have students work in small groups to brainstorm ideas for laws. Then have them work on their own to complete the chart.

- Call on students to share their ideas with the class.

Best Practice

Organizing Information

Graphic organizers such as the one in the Self-Assessment Log teach students how to organize their ideas. This helps students to better assimilate, recall, and explain information at a later date in oral presentations or written assignments.

Self-Assessment Log

- ❑ Read the directions aloud and have students check the strategies and vocabulary they learned in the chapter.

- ❑ Ask a volunteer to tell you where in the chapter information or an activity related to each strategy is located.

- ❑ Tell students to find definitions in the chapter for any words they did not check.

5

Home

In this chapter, students will read about changes that have occurred in family structure over the past millennium. For example, they'll learn about the causes behind the shift from nuclear, or traditional, families to less traditional structures, such as two-parent and blended families. They'll also read about changes that have occurred over the past 800 years in gender roles and in the ways that family members interact with each other. These topics will help students understand connections between social institutions and conventions and events in history.

Chapter Opener

❏ Direct students' attention to the photo and ask questions: *Who are the people in the picture? Where are they? What are they doing?* (This photo is of a family relaxing in their living room.)

❏ Put students in small groups and have them discuss the questions in the **Connecting to the Topic** section.

❏ Read the quotation by Gail Lumet Buckley and ask students what they think it means.

❏ Put this sentence on the board: *I think family is important because _____.* Tell students to complete the sentence with the reasons they think family is important to people's lives. Put students from different language groups in pairs (if possible) to discuss the sentence.

❏ Call on students to share their ideas with the class.

❝ Family faces are magic mirrors. Looking at people who belong to us, we see the past, present and future. ❞

—Gail Lumet Buckley
African American author; daughter of singer Lena Horne (1937–)

Chapter Overview

Reading Skills and Strategies

Recognizing topics in readings about history

Using a timeline to take notes on time and time order

Skimming to find time and place in history

Critical Thinking Skills

Evaluating and predicting family structures and social trends

Vocabulary Building

Recognizing topics in readings about history

Getting meaning from context: punctuation and phrase clues

Recognizing nouns and adjectives

Language Skills

Researching and discussing family structures in different cultures

Focus on Testing

Understanding definitions and explanations

Vocabulary

Nouns		Verbs	Adjectives	Adverb	Preposition
ancestor	housework*	decline	arranged*	modestly*	during*
birthrate	independence*	has (have)	asleep*		
blended families	master*	custody of	communal		
community	meals*	improve*	crowded*		
cooking*	protection*	occur	developing*		
cottage*	relatives*	pushed aside	economic		
decades	single-parent		future		
divorce rate	families		industrialized		
divorces	slaves*		loosely-related		
females*	social* institutions		previous		
fields*	stay-at-home		traditional		
future*	mother		widowed*		
goats*	straw mat		younger*		
history*	structure				
	widows*				
	years*				

* These words are among the 2,000 most-frequently used words in English.

A Short History of the Changing Family

Before You Read

1 Thinking About the Topic

- ❑ Have students look at the photos. Check comprehension by asking questions: *What do these pictures show? How are they similar to each other? How are they different?*

- ❑ Have the students read the questions on page 86 and write brief answers.

- ❑ Put students in small groups to practice asking and answering questions.

- ❑ Call on students to share their answers with the class.

ANSWER KEY

Answers will vary.

2 Predicting

Best Practice

Activating Prior Knowledge

Activities such as this allow students to tap into prior knowledge. Students learn more effectively when new information is meaningful to them, and working in groups to discuss and think about what they already know about a topic will allow students to actively link their prior knowledge to upcoming new information.

- ❑ Put students into small groups to discuss and write answers to the questions. Explain that it is OK to guess if they don't know the answers.

- ❑ Call on students to share their answers with the class.

- ❑ Tell students to look for the answers to the questions in the reading passage as they read.

ANSWER KEY

Answers will vary.

3 Previewing Vocabulary

- ❑ Tell students to look at the list of vocabulary words and repeat them after you read them aloud, or listen and repeat them as you play the tape or CD.

- ❑ Have them put a check mark (✓) next to the words they know.

Read

Content Notes

- ■ The Industrial Revolution occurred between about 1760 and 1830. Before this time, all economies were based on manual labor. But during the Industrial Revolution, much of the manual labor, particularly in Western Europe and North America, was replaced by machines. Before this period, most work was done at home, and husbands and wives shared the work. But industrialization made it necessary for people to work outside the home in factories. So one person from a household had to work outside the home while the other had to stay home and take care of the home and the children. The woman stayed home because she was the one who could breastfeed the children. This major change in lifestyle greatly affected our definitions of gender roles, and this family structure became what is now known as the nuclear family. "Nuclear" in this case refers to the word "nucleus," a core or central point around which other parts are grouped.

- ■ World War II (1939–1945) began as a war between Germany and the Allies, which at first consisted mainly of France, Poland, and the United Kingdom (UK). Later, Italy, Japan, and a few other countries joined Germany, becoming a group called the Axis. Germany invaded the Soviet Union in June of 1941. Then Japan attacked the United States in December of that year, causing the United States to join the Allies. China and a few other countries also eventually joined the Allies. Germany surrendered in May of 1945, and the war ended when Japan surrendered on September 2, 1945. Approximately 62 million people died in World War II, most of them civilians (people not in the military).

■ In 1940, about 10% of working women in America worked in factories. By 1944, that number had jumped to about 30%. The six million American women who went to work in factories during World War II became known as "Rosies," for "Rosie the Riveter." The name comes from the title of a song written in 1943 about these women. A rivet is a metal bolt or pin, and they were used in the building of ships and aircraft for the war.

4 Reading an Article

❑ Have students read the passage silently within a time limit (10–15 minutes), or have students follow along silently as you play the tape or CD.

❑ Tell them to underline any words or phrases that are new or that they don't understand.

After You Read

RECOGNIZING TOPICS IN READINGS ABOUT HISTORY

■ Read the information in the instruction box.

■ Turn to the article "A Short History of the Changing Family" on pages 87–89.

■ Ask students to read the titles of the paragraphs and tell you which paragraphs correspond to the most important ideas of the article, the periods of history, and the final thoughts.

5 Recognizing Topics in a Reading About History

❑ Tell students to look back at the reading passage to find the topic of each paragraph. Have them write their answers on the lines provided.

❑ Call on students to share their answers with the class.

ANSWER KEY

A. family in the past B. different kinds of families
C. changes in the structure of family D. in the 1930s and 1940s E. after World War II; the years
F. in the future; D

 EXPANSION ACTIVITY

■ The aim of this activity is for students to apply the information in the reading to their own lives.

■ Photocopy the Black Line Master **Comparing Families** (BLM 11) and distribute to students.

■ Read the directions.

■ Put students in pairs and have them complete the activity.

■ Call on students to share the similarities and differences that they've identified.

6 Recognizing the Main Idea

Best Practice

Scaffolding Instruction

This activity gives students an opportunity to draw on what they learned in Chapter 4 about identifying the main idea by asking questions. This kind of scaffolded instruction allows students to thoroughly understand one part of a complex concept at a time, in this case finding and understanding the main idea of a reading passage.

❑ Read the directions and explain as needed.

❑ Give students time to complete the first half of the activity as you check their work.

❑ Call on students to share their answers.

❑ Then read the directions for the second half of the activity and change the first sentence to a true statement together as a class. Have two students read item 1 and the true statement that you just wrote as a class.

❑ Give students time to complete the rest of the activity.

❑ Call on students to share their answers.

ANSWER KEY

A. What are the definitions B. What are C. What are the reasons for the D. What happened to E. What changes will happen to F. Were there G. What will families be like

Question about the Whole Reading: have families changed, or has family structure changed

Possible true statements: 1. The nuclear family is different from the extended family: it consists of two parents and their biological or adopted children. 2. There are many kinds of families on Earth today: traditional or nuclear, single-parent, extended, blended, and communal. 3. In the early 1900s in the United States (and later in other countries), the divorce rate went up and the birth rate went down; couples were staying married for fewer years and having fewer children. 4. Before and during World War II, families had serious financial problems in the industrialized world and men were at war, so women had to work outside the home. Families had problems. 5. After the war, family structure changed back in the other direction: there were fewer divorces and more stay-at-home mothers; children began living at home longer. 6. From the 1960s on, there were many new changes in the family. 7. Many people want the traditional two-parent family back; however not many families fall into this category and there may be more single-parent

families, unmarried parents with adopted or foster children, and one-person households.

Strategy

Using a Timeline to Take Notes on Time and Time Order

■ Ask a volunteer to read the Strategy box aloud.

■ To check comprehension, tell students to look at the reading passage and to locate examples of the different ways to identify time.

■ Call on students to share their answers.

7 Identifying Time and Time Order Details

Best Practice

Organizing Information

Activities such as this will teach students to organize information from a reading passage using a graphic organizer. This allows students to better assimilate and recall information at a later date, a valuable study tool. In this case, students place events along a timeline.

❑ Read the directions and copy the timeline on the board.

❑ Do item 1 together as a class. Ask students what time period this sentence describes (1930s to 1940s). Write the number "1" in the box for 1930s to 1940s.

❑ Give students time to complete the activity as you check their work.

❑ Call on students to share their answers. Write their answers in the timeline you drew on the board.

ANSWER KEY

[Across the top] 6, 2, 3, 5

[Across the bottom] 1, 7, 4, 8

8 **Discussing the Reading**

Best Practice

Cultivating Critical Thinking

Activities such as this will help students practice analyzing information and using deductive reasoning. In this activity, students consider the information from the reading and combine it with their own knowledge and ideas about society and the family to develop and share opinions about the reasons for changes in family structure both in the past and in the future.

❑ Put students into small groups to discuss answers to the questions. Ask them to take notes on their discussion.

❑ Call on students to share their answers with the class.

Time with the Family—Past and Present

Before You Read

Strategy

Skimming to Find Time and Place in History

- Tell students to read the information in the Strategy box silently.

- To check comprehension, ask volunteers to skim a few paragraphs in the previous reading and identify the time and place described in each paragraph.

1 **Previewing Vocabulary**

- ❏ Tell students to look at the list of vocabulary words and repeat them after you, or listen and repeat them as you play the tape or CD.

- ❏ Have them put a check mark (✓) next to the words they know.

2 **Skimming**

- ❏ Read the directions.

- ❏ Complete the first item together as a class.

- ❏ Give students time to complete the activity as you check their work.

- ❏ Have students share their answers.

ANSWER KEY

B, C, A, D

3 **Identifying the Main Ideas**

- ❏ Read the directions.

- ❏ Have students read the passage silently and complete the activity within a time limit (10–15 minutes), or have students follow along silently as you play the tape or CD.

- ❏ Tell them to underline any words or phrases that are new or that they don't understand.

- ❏ Call on students to share their answers.

ANSWER KEY

A. A B. C C. B D. B

Read

- ❏ Tell students to read the passage silently within a time limit (10–15 minutes), or have students follow along silently as you play the tape or CD.

After You Read

PARAPHRASING HISTORY TEXTS

- Read the information, paraphrases, and summary in the instruction note aloud as students follow along.

- To check comprehension, ask volunteers to match each sentence in the summary with the corresponding sentences in Paragraph A of the reading.

4 **Writing a Summary**

- ❏ Put students in groups of four and read the directions aloud.

- ❏ Have students summarize their paragraphs and read them aloud to the other members of their groups.

❑ Call on students to read their summaries to the class.

ANSWER KEY

Answers will vary.

5 **Discussing the Reading**

Best Practice

Interacting with Others

These types of collaborative activities help students get a better understanding of the ideas in the reading passage through interacting with other students. They can clarify answers and reinforce knowledge with the assistance of their group members.

❑ Put students into pairs to discuss answers to the questions. Ask them to take notes on their discussion.

❑ Call on students to share their answers with the class.

 EXPANSION ACTIVITY

■ The aim of this activity is for students think critically about the gender roles assigned in most societies today.

■ Photocopy the Black Line Master **Traditional Roles: Pros and Cons** (BLM 12) and distribute to students.

■ Read the directions.

■ Put students in groups of three or four and have them brainstorm ideas together.

■ Call on students to share their group's ideas.

6 **Talking It Over**

❑ Read the directions aloud.

❑ Put students into small groups. Tell them to complete the activity on their own, then share and explain reasons for their answers with their group members.

❑ When students have finished talking with their group members, have one member of each group share their answers and reasons with the class.

Strategy

Getting Meaning from Context: Punctuation and Phrase Clues

- Read the information and the example in the Strategy box aloud.

- To check comprehension, ask volunteers to find these kinds of clues in the reading "Time with the Family—Past and Present" (pages 94–96).

1 Getting Meaning from Context

- ❏ Read the directions aloud.

- ❏ Read the first example and explain if necessary.

- ❏ Have students complete the activity.

- ❏ Call on students to share their answers.

ANSWER KEY

1. from the distant past 2. grandparents, parents, and children, and sometimes aunts, uncles, and cousins 3. parents and their biological or adopted children 4. stays at home and takes care of the children 5. one parent 6. divorced or widowed men and women and their children from previous marriages 7. legal endings to marriage compared to the number of marriages 8. ten years 9. husbands are away at war

Strategy

Recognizing Similar and Opposite Meanings

- Tell students to read the information in the Strategy Box silently. When they are finished, ask volunteers to read the information aloud.

- To check comprehension, write two pairs of words on the board:

    big / large   small / huge

- Ask students how each pair of words belongs together. Do they have similar meanings or opposite meanings? (Pair 1: similar meanings, Pair 2: opposite meanings)

2 Identifying Words with Similar and Opposite Meanings

- ❏ Read the directions aloud and explain the first example.

- ❏ Have students complete the activity as you check their work.

- ❏ Call on students to share their answers.

- ❏ Read and explain the directions below the activity aloud. Tell students that they can use this technique to increase their vocabulary. Model the technique with one or two examples, such as "younger," and "crowded."

ANSWER KEY

1. S 2. O 3. S 4. O 5. S 6. O 7. O 8. O 9. S
10. O 11. O 12. S 13. S 14. O 15. O 16. O 17. S
18. S 19. O 20. O

Strategy

Recognizing Nouns and Adjectives

- Read the information and the example in the Strategy box.

- To check comprehension, copy one or two sentences from the reading on the board and ask students to identify the nouns and adjectives.

3 Identifying Nouns and Adjectives

- ❏ Read the directions aloud and explain the first example. Ask students where the circled words in the example would fit in the chart.

- ❏ Have students complete the activity.

❏ Call on students to share their answers.

❏ Read and explain the directions below the activity aloud. Tell students that they can use this technique to increase their vocabulary.

ANSWER KEY

1. community, family, social 2. human, related, ancestor 3. crowded 4. younger, education 5. arranged marriages, choice 6. history, nuclear 7. widows 8. reason, economic 9. global, industrialization, universal 10. modern, institutions, protection

Chart Answer Key (answers are underlined):

Noun	Related Adjective
community	<u>communal</u>
family	<u>familiar</u>
society	<u>social</u>
relatives	<u>related</u>
ancestors	<u>ancestral</u>
crowd	<u>crowded</u>
youth	<u>younger</u>
<u>arrangement</u>	arranged
<u>marriages</u>	married
<u>history</u>	historical
<u>nucleus</u>	nuclear (family)
<u>widows</u>	widowed
<u>economy</u>	economic
<u>protection</u>	protective

EXPANSION ACTIVITY

■ The aim of this activity is for students to internalize the new vocabulary words.

■ Write the nouns and adjectives (e.g. "community," "communal") from the chart in Activity 3, page 102, on small slips of paper. Give each student a word. Alternatively, include noun/adjective pairs from previous chapters.

■ Have students walk around the room to find the person who has the noun that matches their adjective or vice versa. For example, the student with "community" would look for the student with "communal." Tell them they can ask each person for the match they need, for example, "Do you have *communal*?"

4 Focusing on High-Frequency Words

❏ Read the directions aloud and do the first item as a class.

❏ Have students complete the activity as you circulate and check their progress.

ANSWER KEY

1. straw mat 2. cottage 3. asleep 4. pushed 5. goats 6. cooking 7. housework 8. fields 9. slaves 10. During 11. meals 12. years

5 Making Connections

Best Practice

Making Use of Academic Content

This activity will enable students to better understand the ideas set forth in the reading passage about the changing family. The task of doing an Internet search will help students develop the skills they need to conduct academic research.

❏ If you have access to a computer lab, conduct this activity in the lab so you can help students with their research. Complete it once as a class so students will feel more comfortable doing it again on their own. If you do not have access to a computer lab, assign the activity as homework.

❏ Have students work in pairs to share the information they found.

❏ Call on students to share their research with the class.

UNDERSTANDING DEFINITIONS AND EXPLANATIONS

- Read and explain the information in the instruction note on Understanding Definitions and Explanations.

- Have students complete the activity.

- Call on students to share their answers.

ANSWER KEY

1. C   2. B   3. A   4. C   5. A

 EXPANSION ACTIVITY

- The aim of this activity is for students to internalize the definitions of the new vocabulary words.

- Photocopy the Black Line Master **Vocabulary Bingo** (BLM 13) and distribute to students.

- Read the directions. Write 20–25 vocabulary words on the board for students to choose from. You can use the glossary in the back of the book to find the words or you can have students choose words from the Target Vocabulary in the Self Assessment Log on page 105. Complete a partial Bingo card on the board in order to model two or three examples.

- Model the activity by reading the definitions of two or three words. Be sure to read the definition of at least one word that is not on your card in order to show students that they don't mark anything if the word you define is not on their cards. Have students help you find the correct words on your Bingo card.

- Conduct the game. When a students shouts "Bingo!" check his or her answers. Optional: Give a prize to the winner.

- Note: Be sure to keep track of the words whose definitions you read.

Self-Assessment Log

❏ Read the directions aloud and have students check the strategies and vocabulary they learned in the chapter.

❏ Ask a volunteer to tell you where in the chapter information or an activity related to each strategy is located.

❏ Tell students to find definitions in the chapter for any words they did not check.

6

Cultures of the World

In this chapter, students will read about the concept of culture and all of the elements involved in making up a culture. They will read a conversation among individuals who disagree on what "culture" means and see examples of ways of disagreeing politely. Students will also read anecdotes about cultural misunderstandings that illustrate the importance of understanding a variety of aspects of cultures other than their own. These topics will encourage students to consider different aspects of their own cultures, and possibly create enthusiasm for learning about other cultures.

Chapter Opener

❏ Direct students' attention to the photo and ask questions: *What is interesting about this picture? When and where do you think the picture was taken? How can you tell?* (The photo is of shoppers on a Saturday afternoon at London's famous Portobello Market. London, UK.)

❏ Put students in small groups to discuss the questions in the **Connecting to the Topic** section.

❏ Read the quotation by Mahatma Ghandi and ask students what they think it means.

❏ Put this sentence on the board: *To me, culture means _____.* Tell students to complete the sentence with what the word "culture" means to them. Put students from different language groups in pairs (if possible) to discuss the sentence.

❏ Call on students to share their ideas with the class.

❝ No culture can live, if it attempts to be exclusive. **❞**

—Mahatma Gandhi
nonviolent activist and political leader who helped
lead India to independence (1869–1948)

Chapter Overview

Reading Skills and Strategies

Reading structure: conversation in paragraph form

Recognizing supporting detail: opinions

Understanding anecdotes

Critical Thinking Skills

Interpreting and discussing anecdotes

Summarizing a short story

Vocabulary Building

Understanding new vocabulary in context

Recognizing nouns, verbs, and adjectives

Understanding adverbs of manner

Language Skills

Recognizing and discussing cultural attitudes and customs

Researching and reporting on unfamiliar cultures

Focus on Testing

Practicing vocabulary questions

Vocabulary

Nouns	Verbs	Adjectives	Adverbs
architecture	agree*	amazing	convincingly
attention*	contradict	annoyed*	loudly*
civilization	describe*	clear*	patiently*
contradiction	develop*	enthusiastic	politely*
customer*	experience*	excellent*	rudely*
legacy	greet*	knowing*	
media	invented*	opposing*	
medicine*		pleasant*	
pain*		proud*	
societies*		rude*	
		scientific*	
		social*	
		soft*	
		successful*	
		terrible*	
		tourist*	

* These words are among the 2,000 most-frequently used words in English.

Cross-Cultural Conversation

Content Notes

- Mohandas Karamchand Gandhi was a lawyer educated in England. He became a major spiritual leader of India who encouraged passive resistance, or nonviolence, and used methods such as boycotts and hunger strikes for his cause—India's independence from Great Britain.

- Gandhi was assassinated in 1948 shortly after India gained independence.

- The word "Mahatma" is taken from two Sanskrit words: "maha," which means "great," and "atma," which means "soul." A supporter gave Gandhi that name on January 21, 1925.

Before You Read

1 Previewing the Topic

- Have students look at the picture. Check comprehension by asking a question: *What is happening in the picture?*

- Have the students read the questions and write brief answers.

- Put students in small groups to practice asking and answering questions.

- Call on students to share their answers with the class.

ANSWER KEY
Answers will vary.

2 Predicting

Best Practice

Activating Prior Knowledge

Activities such as this allow students to tap into prior knowledge. Students learn more effectively when new information is meaningful to them, and working in groups to discuss and think about what they already know about a topic will allow students to actively link their prior knowledge to upcoming new information.

- Put students into small groups to discuss and write answers to the questions. Explain that it is OK to guess if they don't know the answers.

- Call on students to share their answers with the class.

- Tell students to look for the answers to the questions in the reading passage as they read.

ANSWER KEY
Answers will vary.

3 Previewing Vocabulary

- Tell students to look at the list of vocabulary words and repeat them after you read them aloud, or listen and repeat them as you play the tape or CD.

- Have them put a check mark (✓) next to the words they know.

ANSWER KEY
Answers will vary.

Read

4 Reading an Article

❑ Have students read the passage silently within a time limit (10–15 minutes), or have students follow along silently as you play the tape or CD.

❑ Tell them to underline any words or phrases that are new or that they don't understand.

After You Read

Best Practice

Organizing Information

Activities such as the one in the following **Expansion Activity** will teach students to organize information using a graphic organizer. This kind of chart allows students to better organize, assimilate, and recall information at a later date, which is a valuable study tool. In this case, students organize information they find on the Internet.

REPRODUCIBLE EXPANSION ACTIVITY

■ The aim of this activity is for students to apply the information in the reading to their own lives.

■ Photocopy the Black Line Master **Achievements of My Culture** (BLM 14) and distribute to students.

■ Read the directions.

■ Have students complete the activity as a class in the computer lab or independently at home.

■ Call on students to share the information they've found.

UNDERSTANDING READING STRUCTURE: CONVERSATION IN PARAGRAPH FORM

■ Read the information in the instruction note.

■ Turn to the article "Cross-Cultural Conversation" on page 109–111.

■ Ask students to identify the speaker in each paragraph.

5 Understanding Reading Structure: Conversation in Paragraph Form

❑ Tell students to look back at the reading passage to find the topic of each paragraph or pair of paragraphs. Have them write their answers on the lines provided.

❑ Call on students to share their answers with the class.

ANSWER KEY

1. the long cultural legacy of the arts in European history 2. humanity's scientific and technological discoveries and achievements 3. the cultural sameness and similarities among modern peoples 4. cultural diversity—how groups vary in their styles and customs 5. polite, friendly ways of discussing ideas and telling opinions
C (All of the speakers are talking about what culture means to them.)

6 Understanding the Point

❑ Read the directions. Do the first item as a class.

❑ Give students time to complete the activity as you check their work.

❑ Call on students to share their answers.

ANSWER KEY

1. Some people believe that a country with a <u>long</u> history has more of a cultural legacy than <u>young</u> countries—especially in its <u>technology and religion</u>. 2. For other thinkers, civilization didn't include old architecture or art; it also meant human <u>scientific and technological discoveries</u> in mathematics, astronomy, medicine, weapons, city building, and the like. 3. Young people around the world <u>want</u> to think about food, media, music, or clothes as culture because those things are <u>modern</u> and <u>everybody</u> seems to like the same kinds. 4. According to others, diversity is <u>more significant than</u> sameness in discussions about culture; such speakers say that people should <u>increase and remember</u> their differences. 5. People from various <u>countries and cultures</u> around the world have <u>different</u> views on the meaning and importance of the concept "culture." In fact, it's common for them to express their ideas in <u>different</u> ways.

RECOGNIZING SUPPORTING DETAIL: OPINIONS

- Ask a volunteer to read the information aloud.

- To check comprehension, tell students to look at the reading passage and to locate examples of italicized words and exclamation points.

---

7 Recognizing Supporting Detail: Opinions

- ❑ Read the directions. Do the first item as a class.

- ❑ Give students time to complete the activity as you check their work.

- ❑ Call on students to share their answers.

ANSWER KEY

1. b, c, e, f 2. b, c, d, e, f 3. c, e, f 4. a, b, c, d, e, f
5. a, b, c, d, e, f

8 Discussing the Reading

Best Practice

Cultivating Critical Thinking

Activities such as this will help students practice analyzing information and determining their own opinions. In this activity, students consider the information from the reading and combine it with their own knowledge and ideas about culture to develop and share opinions about what culture is.

- ❑ Put students into small groups to discuss the answers to the questions. Ask them to take notes on their discussion.

- ❑ Call on students to share their answers with the class.

Clues to World Cultures

Before You Read

1 **Previewing Vocabulary**

- ❑ Tell students to look at the list of vocabulary words and repeat them after you, or have them listen and repeat the words as you play the audio program.

- ❑ Have them put a check mark (✓) next to the words they know.

Read

UNDERSTANDING ANECDOTES

- ▪ Tell students to read the information in the instruction note silently.

- ▪ To check comprehension, ask volunteers some questions about the listed topics. For example, you might ask:
  What are some examples of greetings you use when you meet new people?
  When you are invited to dinner at someone's house, do you bring anything?
  Are there any special rules for eating at someone else's house that a visitor to your culture might not know about?
  What are some examples of gestures and facial expressions specific to your culture?

2 **Reading Stories with Anecdotes**

- ❑ Read the directions.

- ❑ Have students read the passage silently twice and complete the activity within a time limit (20–30 minutes), or have students follow along silently as you play the tape or CD.

- ❑ Tell them to underline any words or phrases that are new or that they don't understand.

- ❑ Call on students to share their answers.

ANSWER KEY

_A_ ideas about individual and group responsibility and rights

_B_ visiting a family at home; eating and drinking with people from other cultures

_C_ body language—gestures, hand movements, and facial expressions

Story A: 1. B 2. B 3. A

Story B: 1. B 2. C 3. A

Story C: 1. A 2. C 3. C

After You Read

3 **Summarizing an Anecdote**

- ❑ Put students in groups and read the directions.

- ❑ Remind students that paraphrasing means to retell in their own words.

- ❑ Tell them to choose one of the anecdotes to summarize.

- ❑ Ask a few volunteers to read their summaries.

4 **Discussing the Reading**

Best Practice

Interacting with Others

These types of collaborative activities help students get a better understanding of the ideas in the reading passage through interacting with other students. They can clarify answers and reinforce knowledge with the assistance of their group members.

- ❑ Put students into small groups to discuss answers to the questions. Ask them to take notes on their discussion.

- ❑ Call on students to share their answers with the class.

ANSWER KEY

Answers will vary.

EXPANSION ACTIVITY

- The aim of this activity is for students to label familiar gestures and expressions, learn some new gestures and expressions, and have fun.

- Mime one or two gestures, such as waving 'hello' or gesturing for someone to come closer and show one or two facial expressions, such as *angry* or *confused* and ask students to guess what you are communicating. Then have volunteers do the same, while the class guesses. Ask students if they know of any gestures from other cultures that their classmates might not know.

5 Talking It Over

- ❏ Read the directions aloud.

- ❏ Put students into small groups. Tell them to complete the activity on their own, then share and explain reasons for their answers with their group members.

- ❏ When students have finished talking with their group members, have one member of each group share their answers and reasons with the class.

Strategy

Understanding New Vocabulary in Context

- Read the information in the Strategy box, and explain as necessary.

- Have students look back at the reading, "Cross-Cultural Conversation" on pages 109–111 and identify the meaning of *culture* that Kamil, Mei, Karen, and Kenji have in mind.

1 Understanding New Vocabulary in Context

- ❏ Read the directions aloud.

- ❏ Read the first example, and explain if necessary. Have students complete the activity.

- ❏ Call on students to share their answers.

ANSWER KEY

Answers will vary. Possible answers:

1. Castles and cathedrals are some examples of old architecture. Some examples of modern architecture are skyscrapers in cities, apartment buildings, museums, schools, etc. / A
2. It began in the Middle East and Africa over five thousand years ago. Civilizations had astronomy, mathematics, medicine, government, and so on. / C
3. A legacy comes from the past. A legacy might include cities, governments, tools, and weapons. / B
4. According to Karen, modern things are part of culture. Karen thinks that people who like classical art and music will disagree with her. Karen and Mei have different opinions. / A
5. Some examples of the worldwide media are movies, TV, CDs, the Internet, newspapers, and magazines. The media gives information, music, and jokes. / C

Best Practice

Scaffolding Instruction

Parts of speech are introduced in this book in a step by step progression. Nouns and adjectives were introduced in Chapter 5, and verbs and adverbs are added in this chapter. This kind of scaffolded instruction allows students to thoroughly understand one part of a complex concept at a time.

Strategy

Recognizing Nouns, Verbs, and Adjectives

- Read the information in the Strategy box.

- To check comprehension, copy one or two sentences from the reading on the board and ask students to identify the nouns, verbs, and adjectives.

2 Recognizing Nouns, Verbs, and Adjectives

- ❏ Read the directions aloud, and explain the first two examples in item 1. Have students complete the third blank in item 1 with you.

- ❏ Have students complete the activity independently.

- ❏ Call on students to share their answers.

ANSWER KEY

1. opposing, opposition, opposed 2. describe, description, descriptive 3. excellence, excel, excellent 4. experienced, experience, experiences 5. civilization, civilize, civilized 6. invent, inventive, inventions 7. agree, agreeable, agreement 8. society, social, socialize 9. contradict, contradictory, contradictions 10. develop, development, developing

EXPANSION ACTIVITY

- The aim of this activity is for students to internalize the new vocabulary words.

- Write the nouns, verbs, and adjectives (e.g. "agreement," "agree," agreeable") from Activity 2 on small slips of paper. Give each student a word. Alternatively, include noun/verb/adjective trios from previous chapters.

- Have students walk around the room to find the two people who have the words that match theirs. For example, the student with "agreement" would look for the student with "agree" and "agreeable."

UNDERSTANDING ADVERBS OF MANNER

- Read the information in the instruction note.

- To check comprehension, ask students for examples of adverbs.

3 Using Adverbs and Adjectives of Manner

- Read the directions aloud, and explain item 1.

- Have students complete the activity.

- Call on students to share their answers.

- Choose a word from Chapters 1–6 and as a class have students identify the related forms (for example, Ch 1: instructor, instruct, instructional; requirement, require, required).

ANSWER KEY

1. proudly, patient 2. clear, pleasant 3. knowing, rudely 4. enthusiastic, amazingly 5. loudly
6. scientific 7. successful 8. politely 9. soft
10. enthusiastic, convincingly

4 Focusing on High-Frequency Words

- Read the directions aloud, and do the first item as a class.

- Have students complete the activity as you circulate and check their progress.

ANSWER KEY

1. tourist 2. terrible 3. medicine 4. customer
5. patiently 6. attention 7. greet 8. pain
9. loudly 10. annoyed 11. rudely

5 Making Connections

Best Practice

Making Use of Academic Content

Activities such as this provide students with practice researching topics on the Internet. This skill will be useful in a variety of academic contexts.

- If you have access to a computer lab, conduct this activity in the lab so you can help students with their research. Complete the activity once as a class so students feel more comfortable doing the activity on their own. If you do not have access to a computer lab, assign this activity as homework.

- Have students work in pairs to share the information they found.

- Call on students to share their research findings with the class.

TOEFL® IBT

PRACTICING VOCABULARY QUESTIONS

- Read and explain the information in the instruction note.

- To check comprehension, have students turn to Paragraph B of "Cross-Cultural Conversation" on page 109–111. Write the following on the board:

  Which of the following is closest in meaning to "agree," as it is used in Paragraph B?

  a. to have a different opinion
  b. a different opinion
  c. to have the same opinion
  d. a similar opinion

- Read the directions, and explain as necessary.

- Have students complete the activity.

- Call on students to share their answers.

ANSWER KEY

1. C   2. D   3. A   4. C   5. B

 EXPANSION ACTIVITY

- The aim of this activity is for students to examine the concept of culture and what it means to them, and to practice both developing a consensus and disagreeing politely.

- Photocopy the Black Line Master **What Makes a Culture?** (BLM 15) and distribute to students.

- Read the directions.

- Have students complete the activity in groups of three.

- Call on students to share and explain the reasoning behind their rankings.

Self-Assessment Log

- Read the directions aloud and have students check the strategies and vocabulary they learned in the chapter.

- Ask a volunteer to tell you where in the chapter information or an activity related to each strategy is located.

- Tell students to find definitions in the chapter for any words they did not check.

7

Health

In this chapter, students will read about populations that claim remarkable longevity. They will learn about the diet, habits, and lifestyle characteristics that these groups share, and the ways in which they differ. Students will also read about modern beliefs about health and nutrition, both facts and opinions, about the effect that the Internet has had on health education over the years, and about DNA and genetic technology. The second reading begins to weigh the pros and cons of medical information found on the Internet and of the claims of genetic technology. These readings will encourage students to think about their own lifestyles and habits and how they relate to the lifestyles and habits of other people around the world.

Chapter Opener

❑ Direct students' attention to the photo and ask the questions: *What is interesting about this picture? How would you describe the people in the photo? What do you think their lifestyle is like?* (The photo is of a couple hiking.)

❑ Put students in groups and have them discuss the questions in the **Connecting to The Topic** section.

❑ Read the Arabian proverb and ask students what they think it means.

❑ Put this sentence on the board: *Healthy people _____.* Tell students to complete the sentence with a description of healthy people—what they're like, what they do. Put students from different language groups in pairs (if possible) to discuss the sentence.

❑ Call on students to share their ideas with the class.

❝ He who has health has hope, and he who has hope has everything. ❞

—Arabian proverb

Chapter Overview

Reading Skills and Strategies

Recognizing reading structure using a mind map

Understanding the main idea

Understanding facts and opinions

Recognizing supporting details after punctuation, numbers, and connecting words

Critical Thinking Skills

Choosing information to complete a mind map

Summarizing using a mind map

Vocabulary Building

Figuring out new or difficult vocabulary

Identifying synonyms

Identifying part of speech from suffixes

Language Skills

Giving advice about health

Evaluating and agreeing or disagreeing with health tips

Focus on Testing

Practicing for timed readings

Vocabulary

Nouns		Verbs	Adjectives
claims*	genes	correct*	accurate
combination*	inhabitants	oppose*	dishonest*
cure*	length*	prevent*	elderly*
damage*	longevity	solve*	famous*
decisions*	patients		genetic
disease*	population*		long-lived
engineering*	streams*		moderate*
environment			proven*
			sour*
			unpolluted
			valid

*These words are among the 2,000 most-frequently used words in English.

The Secrets of a Very Long Life

Before You Read

1 Previewing the Topic

- ❑ Have students look at the photo. Check comprehension by asking a question: *What is happening in the picture?*

- ❑ Have the students read the questions and write brief answers.

- ❑ Put students in small groups to practice asking and answering questions.

- ❑ Call on students to share their answers with the class.

2 Predicting

> #### Best Practice
>
> **Activating Prior Knowledge**
>
> Activities such as this allow students to tap into their prior knowledge. Students learn more effectively when new information is meaningful to them, and working in groups to discuss and think about what they already know about a topic will allow students to actively link their prior knowledge to upcoming new information.

- ❑ Put students into small groups to discuss and write answers to the questions. Explain that it is OK to guess if they don't know the answers.

- ❑ Call on students to share their answers with the class.

- ❑ Tell students to look for the answers to the questions in the reading passage as they read.

ANSWER KEY

Answers will vary.

3 Previewing Vocabulary

- ❑ Tell students to look at the list of vocabulary words and repeat them after you read them aloud, or listen and repeat them as you play the tape or CD.

- ❑ Have them put a check mark (✓) next to the words they know.

Read

> ### Content Notes
>
> - ■ Average life expectancy for people born in the United States in 1901 was 49 years. By 2000, life expectancy was 77 years. This rise is due to better public health, nutrition, and medicine. But because these numbers are averages, the biggest factor in the increase is a significant drop in infant death rates.
>
> - ■ Some recent average life expectancy rates:
>   North America: 75 + years
>   Australia: 75 + years
>   South America: 70 + years
>   Central America: 75 + years
>   Western Europe: 75 + years
>   Northern Africa: 70 + years
>   Sub-Saharan Africa: 59 years and below
>   Asia: 70 +
>   Southern Asia: 60 +
>   Southeast Asia: 60 +

4 Reading an Article

- ❑ Have students read the passage silently within a time limit (10–15 minutes), or have students follow along silently as you play the tape or CD.

- ❑ Tell them to underline any words or phrases that are new or that they don't understand.

After You Read

Strategy

Recognizing Reading Structure Using a Mind Map

- Read the information in the Strategy box.

- Have students look at the mind map in Activity 5 on page 136.

- Ask students to match each bullet in the box with a circle or set of circles on the mind map.

Best Practice

Organizing Information

Activities such as the following two (Activities 5 and 6) will teach students to organize information using a graphic organizer. This kind of chart will allow students to better organize, assimilate, and recall information at a later date, which is a valuable study tool. In this case, students first read a completed mind map, and then they complete a similar mind map.

5 Recognizing Reading Structure Using a Mind Map

- Have students complete the activity as you check their progress.

- Call on students to share their answers with the class.

ANSWER KEY

1. A Mind Map of Paragraph B 2. Examples, Reasons 3. Unusual Longevity, New fathers at 90, Women give birth at 50 4. three, Unpolluted environment; A simple, nutritious diet; Physical work and activity 5. Clean air, Clean water 6. 5, vitamins, fiber, low fat and cholesterol, not much sugar, no unnatural chemicals 7. Physical work and activity

EXPANSION ACTIVITY

- The aim of this activity is for students to examine the concept of life expectancy and relate it to their own lives.

- Photocopy the Black Line Master **Comparing Lifestyles and Researching Life Expectancy** (BLM 16) and distribute to students.

- Read the directions.

- Have students complete the activity.

- Call on students to share their Venn diagrams and their life expectancy rates.

6 Completing a Mind Map

- Read the directions. Do the first item as a class.

- Give students time to complete the activity as you check their work.

- Copy the mind map on the board. Call on students to share their answers. Fill in the mind map as students give their answers.

ANSWER KEY

In circles under "1. Places where people live..." The Caucasus Mountains in Russia; Vilcabamba, Ecuador

In box above "2. Diets of the 3 regions Differences" 2. Hunzukut diet: raw vegetables, fruit, chapatis 3. Ecuadorian diet: grain, vegetables, fruit, coffee, alcohol, cigarettes

In box below "2. Diets of the 3 regions Similarities" 2. Fewer calories 3. traditional herbs and medicines (in box below "3. Other possible causes...") 2. Stress-free lives 3. Physical work and other activities 4. Extended family structure

B. some possible secrets of the mystery of longevity

In circle below "4. Disbelief in claims about longevity" No valid birth certificates

7 **Understanding the Main Idea**

❑ Read the directions, and explain as necessary.

❑ Give students time to complete the activity as you check their work.

❑ Call on students to share their answers.

ANSWER KEY

Answers will vary. Possible answers:

Main-idea question: Why do people in some areas of the world live for a very long time?

According to health specialists that <u>study</u> longevity, there are <u>some</u> possible reasons for a <u>long</u> and <u>healthy</u> life. The first requirement might be a high level of hard <u>physical</u> work and activity <u>with</u> freedom from modern worries. Second, the physical environment makes <u>a lot of</u> difference: people seem to live longer in a <u>high mountain</u> region with a <u>steady</u> climate of <u>moderate</u> air temperatures. And finally, diet <u>is very important</u>: long-lived people seem to eat mostly foods high in <u>vitamins and nutrition</u> but low in <u>fat, cholesterol, and sugar</u>.

Strategy

Recognizing Supporting Details after Punctuation, Numbers, and Connecting Words

■ Ask a volunteer to read the information in the Strategy box aloud.

■ To check comprehension, tell students to look at the reading passage and to locate examples of colons, parenthetical numbers, and connecting words and phrases.

■ When students find connecting words and phrases in the reading passage, ask them to identify what the connector is doing. For example, is it introducing an addition or similarity, a contrast or contradiction, or a cause, reason, or result?

8 **Recognizing Supporting Details After Punctuation, Numbers, and Connecting Words**

❑ Read the directions. Do the first item as a class.

❑ Give students time to complete the activity as you check their work.

❑ Call on students to share their answers.

ANSWER KEY

Answers will vary. Possible answers:

1. Medical scientists and health specialists might want to travel to these regions to solve the mystery of longevity and bring these secrets to the modern world. 2. The three reasons for the good health of the people of Hunza are a healthful, unpolluted environment; a simple diet high in vitamins, fiber, and nutrition but low in fat, cholesterol, sugar, and chemicals; and physical work and activities. 3. These two people were Shirali and his widow. 4. The people of the Caucasus Mountains almost never get sick and they don't lose their hair, teeth, or eyesight. 5. In Vilcabamba, the environment is clean and beautiful, the climate is always moderate, the water is high in minerals, and there are a lot of flowers, fruits, vegetables, and wildlife. 6. All the food is natural, people don't eat many calories, and people use traditional herbs and medicines. 7. Other reasons for these people's health and longevity are physical activity, no stress, and an extended family structure. 8. Some doctors don't believe the longevity claims because these groups of people don't keep official government birth records, and they think that human life has a natural limit of about 110 years.

9 Discussing the Reading

Cultivating Critical Thinking

Activities such as this will help students practice analyzing information and determining their own opinions. In this activity, students consider the information from the reading and combine it with their own knowledge to discuss the possibility of extreme longevity—their own and that of the people they just read about.

❏ Put students into small groups to discuss answers to the questions. Ask them to take notes on their discussion.

❏ Call on students to share their answers with the class.

Claims to Amazing Health

Before You Read

1 **Previewing Vocabulary**

- ❏ Tell students to look at the list of vocabulary words and repeat them after you, or listen and repeat them as you play the tape or CD.

- ❏ Have them put a check mark (✓) next to the words they know.

Read

Content Notes

- ■ The Swiss scientist Friedrich Miescher first isolated DNA in 1869. He called the white chemical that he found "nuclein." He didn't know what it contained.

- ■ By the 1940s, scientists knew what DNA was made of: phosphate, sugar, and four chemicals. But they didn't know what DNA looked like.

- ■ In 1953, James Watson, an American scientist, and Francis Crick, a British researcher, published a paper explaining that DNA looked like a double helix: two chains of molecules shaped like a spiral staircase. In 1962, Watson and Crick received the Nobel prize for their discovery.

2 **Understanding Facts and Opinions**

- ❏ Read the directions, and explain as necessary.

- ❏ Use examples to illustrate the difference between fact and opinion. For example, write the following sentences on the board: *Oranges have a lot of vitamin C. Oranges taste better than apples.* Ask students to say which is a fact and which is an opinion.

- ❏ Ask students for other examples of facts and opinions.

- ❏ Have students read the passage silently twice and answer the questions within a time limit (20–30 minutes), or have students follow along silently as you play the tape or CD.

- ❏ Tell them to underline any words or phrases that are new or that they don't understand.

- ❏ Call on students to share their answers.

ANSWER KEY

Paragraph A: C, A Paragraph B: B, C Paragraph C: A, B Paragraph D: A, B

After You Read

Strategy

Summarizing Using a Mind Map

- ■ Ask a volunteer to read the information in the Strategy box aloud.

- ■ To check comprehension, and to help students see the relationship between the mind map and the summary, ask students to match sentences in the summary with information in the mind map.

Best Practice

Interacting with Others

Collaborative activities such as Activities 3 and 4 help students get a better understanding of the ideas in the reading passage through interacting with other students. They can clarify answers and reinforce knowledge with the assistance of their group members.

3 Summarizing Using a Mind Map

- ❑ Put students in groups of three, and read the directions aloud.

- ❑ Have each student choose and summarize a paragraph using a mind map, and read their summaries aloud to the other members of their groups.

- ❑ Call on students to read their summaries to the class.

ANSWER KEY

Answers may vary.

4 Discussing the Reading

- ❑ Put students into small groups to discuss answers to the questions. Ask them to take notes on their discussion.

- ❑ Call on students to share their answers with the class.

EXPANSION ACTIVITY

REPRODUCIBLE

- ■ The aim of this activity is for students to practice doing Internet research and to practice skimming for information.

- ■ Photocopy the Black Line Master **Internet Search: Diseases and Cures** (BLM 17) and distribute to students.

- ■ Read the directions.

- ■ Have students complete the activity.

- ■ Call on students to share the information they found.

5 Talking It Over

- ❑ Read the directions aloud.

- ❑ Put students into small groups. Tell them to complete the activity on their own, then share and explain reasons for their answers with their group members.

- ❑ You can also assign the research portion of the activity as homework, asking students to research at least three of the situations before coming to class to discuss them.

- ❑ When students have finished talking with their group members, have one member of each group share their answers and reasons with the class.

Strategy

Getting Meaning from Context

- Read the information in the Strategy box, and explain as necessary.

- Remind students of what they learned in Chapter 6 about understanding the meanings of new words from context.

- Review some of the strategies students can use to understand new words from context if definitions and explanations and parts of speech are not included, such as figuring out what part of speech it is, and looking at the other words near it.

1   Figuring Out New or Difficult Vocabulary

- ❏ Read the directions aloud, and explain if necessary.

- ❏ Do the various parts of item 1 together as a class. Have students complete the activity.

- ❏ Call on students to share their answers.

- ❏ Read and explain the directions below the activity aloud. Tell students that they can use this technique to increase their vocabulary. The suggested words are found in the reading on pages 133–135: (*benefits*: Paragraph B; *preservatives*: Paragraph E; *an average*: Paragraph E; *stress*: Paragraph F).

ANSWER KEY

Possible answers:

1. health specialists, they want to know how other people might live as long as these people, they're studying people who live past 100 years, C, A 2. clean air and water and moderate temperatures, the land, air, and water in an area, D, very hot or very cold, B 3. they were inhabitants, people, A, D 4. no, a lot of minerals, water from high mountain streams, D, A
5. people, C, no, valid birth records, A, yes, yes, D

2   Identifying Synonyms

- ❏ Read the directions aloud, and explain the first item.

- ❏ Have students complete the activity.

- ❏ Call on students to share their answers.

ANSWER KEY

1. d 2. a 3. i 4. g 5. c 6. j 7. f 8. k 9. b 10. h 11. e

Best Practice

Scaffolding Instruction

Parts of speech are introduced in this book in a step-by-step progression. Nouns and adjectives were introduced in Chapter 5, Verbs and Adverbs in Chapter 6, and suffixes for particular parts of speech are added in this chapter. This kind of scaffolded instruction allows students to thoroughly understand one part of a complex concept at a time.

RECOGNIZING PARTS OF SPEECH FROM WORD ENDINGS: SUFFIXES

- Read the information in the instruction note.

- To check comprehension, write several words from the chart on the board and ask students to identify their parts of speech.

- Then write some adjectives (responsible, active, agreeable) on the board and ask students for a corresponding noun (responsibility, activity/action, agreement).

3   Identifying Parts of Speech from Suffixes

- ❏ Read the directions aloud, and explain the examples.

- ❏ Have students complete the activity.

- ❏ Call on students to share their answers.

- ❏ If you wish, read the directions below the list and have students write five sentences each.

ANSWER KEY

1. _n_ ability
2. _adj_ active
3. _adv_ actively
4. _n_ activity
5. _n_ agreement
6. _adj_ agreeable
7. _adv_ agreeably
8. _adj_ biological
9. _adj_ believable
10. _adj_ beneficial
11. _adj_ changeable
12. _adj_ convenient
13. _n_ disappearance
14. _adv_ forward
15. _n_ longevity
16. _adj_ magnificent
17. _n_ politeness
18. _n_ prevention
19. _adj_ preventive
20. _n_ production
21. _adj_ religious
22. _n_ requirements
23. _n_ residence
24. _adj_ returnable
25. _adj_ sensible
26. _adv_ similarly
27. _adj_ supportive
28. _n_ television
29. _adj_ theoretical
30. _adj_ visual

REPRODUCIBLE — EXPANSION ACTIVITY

- The aim of this activity is for students to internalize the new suffixes.

- Make one photocopy of the Black Line Master **Find Your Match** (BLM 18). Cut out the individual slips.

- Give each student a slip of paper.

- Have students walk around the room to find a person with a root form or suffix that fits theirs. For example, the student with "agree" would look for the student with "ment" or "able." The student with "resid-" would look for the student with "ent" or "ence".

- When students find their matches, have them write down the word they made, and the person who had the root word or suffix to fit theirs.

4 Choosing Word Forms with Suffixes

- ❑ Read the directions aloud, and explain item 1.
- ❑ Have students complete the activity.
- ❑ Call on students to share their answers.

ANSWER KEY

1. mountainous, famous, longevity, various
2. scientific, physical, reason, pollution, environment 3. naturally, nutritious, beneficial, advantageous 4. usually, active, activity, movement 5. especially, available, agreement, generally 6. typical, mostly, mainly, traditional
7. important, environment, confusion, validity
8. available, information, combination, cultural
9. ignorant, medical, decisions, recommendations
10. value, genetic, defective, biological

Parts of Speech		
Noun	**Adjective**	**Adverb**
advantages	advantageous	X
availability	_available_	X
activity	active	actively
biology	biological	biologically
confusion	confused	X
culture	cultural	culturally
defects	defective	X
decisions	decisive	decisively
fame	famous	famously
genes	genetic	genetically
generalities	general	generally
humanity	human	humanely
ignorance	ignorant	ignorantly
importance	important	importantly
nature	natural	naturally
mountains	mountainous	X
type	typical	_typically_
tradition	traditional	traditionally

5 **Focusing on High-Frequency Words**

- ❏ Read the directions aloud, and do the first item as a class.

- ❏ Have students complete the activity as you circulate and check their progress.

ANSWER KEY

1. combination 2. diseases 3. parents 4. correct
5. improve 6. damage 7. improve 8. oppose
9. engineering

6 **Making Connections**

Best Practice

Making Use of Academic Content

Activities such as this will enable students to better understand the ideas set forth in the reading passage about the changing family. The task of doing an Internet search will allow students to develop the skills they need to conduct academic research.

- ❏ If you have access to a computer lab, conduct this activity in the lab so you can help students with their research. Complete the activity once as a class so students feel more comfortable doing the activity on their own. If you do not have access to a computer lab, assign this activity as homework.

- ❏ Have students work in pairs to share the information they found.

- ❏ Call on students to share their research with the class.

FOCUSING ON TIMED READINGS AND NOTE-TAKING

- Read and explain the information in the instruction note.

- To check comprehension, ask questions like *What should you concentrate on as you read? What should you do with difficult questions? Can you read the passage more than once? Is it important to spell words correctly in your notes?*

- Have students complete the activity.

- Call on students to share their answers.

- Read the instructions, and tell students they will have 20 minutes to read the passage and answer the questions.

- Tell students that if they finish before the time is up, they can go back and check the answers they are unsure of.

- Go over the answers as a class.

ANSWER KEY

1. A 2. B 3. D 4. C 5. B 6. D

EXPANSION ACTIVITY

- The aim of this activity is for students to gather and analyze simple data.

- Ask how many students exercise ten or more hours a week, six to ten hours a week, three to six hours a week, one to three hours a week, thirty minutes to an hour a week, and not at all. Tally their answers on the board.

- Draw a simple column graph on the board. On the vertical axis, write the numbers 1–10 with one at the bottom.

- On the horizontal axis, write "10 hours," "6–10 hours," "3–6 hours," "1–3 hours," "1/2–1 hour," and "0–1/2 hour."

- Have students help you complete the column graph with the tallied information you wrote on the board. For example, if three students exercise ten or more hours a week, draw a bar from the horizontal axis up to the number "3" on the vertical axis.

- Ask students how the amount of exercise they get compares with the physical activity of our ancient ancestors described in the reading passage.

Self-Assessment Log

- ❑ Read the directions aloud and have students check the strategies and vocabulary they learned in the chapter.

- ❑ Ask a volunteer to tell you where in the chapter information or an activity related to each strategy is located.

- ❑ Tell students to find definitions in the chapter for any words they did not check.

8

Entertainment and the Media

In this chapter, students will read about the visual media. They will learn some advantages of visual media, such as the improvement in thinking that can occur from watching certain kinds of high-quality programming, as well as some disadvantages, such as its potential to reduce people's ability to concentrate. Students will also read and summarize plots of movies and television shows. These readings will encourage students to think about how they might be affected by the visual media that surrounds them every day.

Chapter Opener

- ❏ Direct students' attention to the photo and ask questions: *Where are these people? What are they doing?* (This photo was taken in a TV studio. It is of TV producers filming a talk show.)

- ❏ Put students in groups and have them discuss the questions in the **Connecting to The Topic** section.

- ❏ Read the quote by Samuel I. Hayakawa and ask students what they think it means.

- ❏ Put this sentence on the board: *I watch _____ hours of television a day. I think TV is good/bad because _____.* Tell students to complete the sentences with the number of hours of TV they watch per day and their opinion about TV. Put students from different language groups in pairs (if possible) to discuss the sentence.

- ❏ Call on students to share their ideas with the class.

❝ In the age of television, image becomes more important than substance. ❞

—Samuel I. Hayakawa
Semanticist, Educator, and U.S. Senator (1906–1992)

Chapter Overview

Reading Skills and Strategies

Recognizing reading structure: using an outline

Understanding the point and recognizing supporting details

Putting events in order

Critical Thinking Skills

Completing an outline with reading material

Classifying different types of stories

Evaluating the advantages and disadvantages of the media

Summarizing a story

Vocabulary Building

Understanding suffixes (nouns, adverbs, adjectives)

Understanding word families

Language Skills

Retelling a story plot

Discussing and justifying media choices

Persuading others to watch a particular show

Focus on Testing

Focusing on comparison and contrast

Vocabulary

Nouns	Verbs	Adjectives	
addiction	concentrate	addicted	exciting*
adulthood	envy*	aural	immoral
adults	improve*	bloody*	natural*
behavior*	investigate	boring	nursing*
concentration	practice*	computerized	reality
hospitals*	replace*	dissatisfied*	scary
personalities*	scare	elderly*	shadowy*
programming*		emotional	suspenseful
reality*		envious	unlimited*
relationship*			
stars*			
viewers			
violence*			
visual media			

*These words are among the 2,000 most-frequently used words in English.

How the Visual Media Affect People

Before You Read

1 Previewing the Topic

- ❑ Have students look at the photos. Check comprehension by asking a question: *What is happening in the pictures?*

- ❑ Have the students read the questions and write brief answers.

- ❑ Put students in small groups to practice asking and answering questions.

- ❑ Call on students to share their answers with the class.

2 Predicting

> **Best Practice**
>
> **Activating Prior Knowledge**
>
> Activities such as this allow students to tap into prior knowledge. Students learn more effectively when new information is meaningful to them, and working in groups to discuss and think about what they already know about a topic will allow students to actively link their prior knowledge to upcoming new information.

- ❑ Put students into small groups to discuss and write answers to the questions. Explain that it is OK to guess if they don't know the answers.

- ❑ Call on students to share their answers with the class.

- ❑ Tell students to look for the answers to the questions in the reading passage as they read.

ANSWER KEY

Answers will vary.

3 Previewing Vocabulary

- ❑ Tell students to look at the list of vocabulary words and repeat them after you read them aloud, or listen and repeat them as you play the tape or CD.

- ❑ Have them put a check mark (✓) next to the words they know.

Read

> **Content Notes**
>
> - The average American watches over 28 hours of TV per week.
>
> - 99% of American homes have at least one TV, with an average of 2.24 TVs per household.
>
> - 66% of American homes have three or more TV sets.
>
> - Americans watch 250 billion hours of TV a year.
>
> - The average American will see 200,000 violent acts, including 40,000 murders, on TV by the age of 18.
>
> Source: http://www.csun.edu/~vceed002/health/docs/ tv&health.html#tv_stats

4 Reading an Article

- ❑ Have students read the passage silently within a time limit (15–20 minutes), or have students follow along silently as you play the tape or CD.

- ❑ Tell them to underline any words or phrases that are new or that they don't understand.

After You Read

Strategy

Recognizing Reading Structure: Using an Outline

- Read the information in the Strategy box.

- To help clarify the information, write this outline on the board:
  Topic
      I. Main idea
        A. Supporting detail
          1. More details
          2. More details

        B. Supporting detail
          1. More details
          2. More details

        C. Supporting detail
          1. More details
          2. More details

      II. Main idea
        A. Supporting detail
          1. More details
          etc.

5 Completing an Outline

Best Practice

Organizing Information

Activities such as this one will teach students to organize information using a graphic organizer. This kind of outline allows students to better organize, assimilate, and recall information at a later date, a valuable study tool. In this case, students complete an outline of the reading passage.

- ❏ Have students complete the activity as you check their progress.

- ❏ Call on students to share their answers with the class.

ANSWER KEY

Answers will vary. Possible answers:

What is the topic? —How the visual media affect people

What are the two main ideas about the topic? —Advantages of visual media, Disadvantages of visual media

I. Advantages
  A. Increase people's knowledge and thinking ability (A)
  B. Benefit the elderly and the sick (A)
  C. Provide language learners instruction and practice (A)
  D. Offer good entertainment for free time (A)

II. Disadvantages
  A. Take too much time from family life and other activities (B)
  B. Reduce people's ability to concentrate, focus, or reason (C)
  C. Scare people or get them used to violence (D)
  D. Cause dissatisfaction in normal people's lives (E) and (F)
  E. Addict people to TV and video (G)

 EXPANSION ACTIVITY

- The aim of this activity is for students to examine their own exposure to the visual media.

- Photocopy the Black Line Master **Visual Media Journal** (BLM 19) and distribute to students.

- Read the directions.

- Have students complete the activity over a two-day period.

- Call on students to share the information from their journals.

6 **Understanding the Point and Recognizing Supporting Detail**

❑ Read the directions, and explain as necessary.

❑ Give students time to complete the activity as you check their work.

❑ Call on students to share their answers.

ANSWER KEY

Answers will vary. Possible answers:

Main-idea question: What are some positive and negative features of <u>the visual media</u>?

[A] Television and other visual media probably influence people's lives in <u>positive and negative</u> ways. Here are examples of their possible benefits: (1) <u>High-quality</u> programming in various fields provides educational value to <u>average and well-educated people</u>. It can <u>improve</u> thinking ability. (2) Also, elderly and sick people who rarely go out <u>can</u> enjoy TV, videotapes, or DVDs. (3) <u>Additionally</u>, students get <u>a lot of</u> educational benefit from shows in the languages they are trying to learn. (4) Another advantage is that TV can help people to <u>relax</u> in their free time at home.

[B] <u>Nevertheless</u>, there are serious disadvantages to the visual media: (1) An "electronic baby-sitter" is likely to <u>replace family communication</u> and <u>reduce</u> the amount of time they spend on other activities. (2) Second, too much television or work on a computer may make it <u>harder</u> for the overly relaxed brain to pay attention, concentrate, or reason. (3) Third, violent or horrible TV images and language can give frequent viewers <u>nightmares</u>, making them fearful of <u>the images and language</u>; or people may begin to think of terrible events or acts as <u>normal</u>. (4) A fourth possible disadvantage of too much television, video, and other kinds of visual media is that people may become <u>dissatisfied</u> with the reality of their <u>normal</u> lives. (5) And finally, the most negative effect of the visual media is probably viewer <u>addiction</u>. TV and video watchers <u>won't</u> be able to get away from the media easily; they can <u>easily</u> become addicted.

7 **Discussing the Reading**

Best Practice

Cultivating Critical Thinking

Activities such as this will help students practice analyzing information and determining their own opinions. In this activity, students consider the information from the reading and combine it with their own knowledge to discuss the advantages and disadvantages of the visual media.

❑ Put students into small groups to discuss answers to the questions. Ask them to take notes on their discussion.

❑ Call on students to share their answers with the class.

Media Stories

Before You Read

1 Previewing Vocabulary

- ❏ Tell students look at the list of vocabulary words and repeat them after you, or listen and repeat them as you play the audio program.

- ❏ Have them put a check mark (✓) next to the words they know.

2 Classifying Stories and Putting Events in Order

- ❏ Read the directions, and explain as necessary.

- ❏ Ask students for examples of each kind of story (movies or TV shows).

- ❏ Have students skim the passage silently and complete the activity.

- ❏ Call on students to share their answers.

ANSWER KEY

Answers may vary. Possible answers:

1. B and C 2. A 3. — 4. D 5. A 6. C 7. —
8. — 9. — 10. —

Read

Content Note

- ■ Sir Alfred Hitchcock was a famous and successful film director and producer. He specialized in suspense thrillers and horror films. Many people consider *Psycho* to be one of Alfred Hitchcock's best films. Many also consider it one of the best horror films ever made.

3 Finding the Main Idea

- ❏ Read the directions, and explain as necessary.

- ❏ Have students read the passage silently and complete the activity within a time limit (20–30 minutes), or have students follow along silently as you play the tape or CD.

- ❏ Tell them to underline any words or phrases that are new or that they don't understand.

- ❏ Call on students to share their answers.

ANSWER KEY

Story Plot A: B Story Plot B: A Story Plot C: C
Story Plot D: B

After You Read

Strategy

Summarizing a Story

- ■ Have students read the information and example in the Strategy box silently.

- ■ To check comprehension, have students use the *Psycho* plot in Story Plot A on page 168 to help you write a summary on the board.

4 Summarizing a Story

- ❏ Put students in groups of three, and read the directions aloud.

- ❏ Have each student choose and summarize a story and read their summaries aloud to the other members of their groups.

- ❏ Call on students to read their summaries to the class.

ANSWER KEY

Answers will vary.

Best Practice

Interacting with Others

Collaborative activities such as Activity 5 and the following Expansion Activity help students get a better understanding of the ideas in the reading passage through interacting with other students. They can clarify their ideas and reinforce knowledge with the assistance of their group members.

5 Discussing the Reading

❑ Put students into small groups to discuss answers to the questions. Ask them to take notes on their discussion.

❑ Call on students to share their answers with the class.

EXPANSION ACTIVITY

■ The aim of this activity is for students to practice organizing and telling short narratives.

■ Tell students that they will have one minute to describe a movie or TV show that they think most of their classmates know and their classmates are going to guess what the movie or TV show is.

■ Give students 10–15 minutes to write a short summary of the movie or TV show they want to describe.

■ Give each student one minute to share their summary. Then have students guess the movie or TV show.

6 Talking It Over

❑ Read the directions aloud.

❑ Put students into small groups. Tell them to complete the activity on their own, then share and explain reasons for their answers with their group members.

❑ You can also assign the research portion of the activity as homework, asking students to research at least three of the situations before coming to class to discuss them.

❑ When students have finished talking with their group members, have one member of each group share their answers and reasons with the class.

Strategy

Getting Meaning from Context

- Read the information, and explain as necessary.

- Remind students that they practiced this strategy in chapters 6 and 7.

- Review the Strategy boxes on pages 120 and 147 if necessary.

1 **Understanding New Vocabulary from Context**

- Read the directions aloud, and explain if necessary.

- Do the first item as a class.

- Call on students to share their answers.

- Read and explain the directions below the activity aloud. Tell students that they can use this technique to increase their vocabulary. (*visual*: title; *action programming*: Paragraph D; *likely*: Paragraph D; *normal*: Paragraph E ; *boring*: Paragraph F; *truthful*: Paragraph G)

ANSWER KEY

1. (I.C.) aural comprehension = B 2. (I.B.) elderly = B, nursing facilities = D 3. (I.A.) programming = C 4. (I.D.) entertainment = B 5. (II.B.) concentrate = A, deficit = C 6. (II.A.) replace = A 7. (II.C.) violence = B, nightmares = A 8. (II.D.) trash TV = B, stars = D, immoral = A

Best Practice

Scaffolding Instruction

Parts of speech are introduced in this book in a step-by-step progression. Nouns and adjectives were introduced in Chapter 5, Verbs and Adverbs in Chapter 6, and suffixes for particular parts of speech are added in Chapter 7. The topic of suffixes is continued in this chapter. This kind of scaffolded instruction allows students to thoroughly understand one part of a complex concept at a time.

UNDERSTANDING SUFFIXES

- Read the information in the instruction note.

- To check comprehension, ask students for examples of words that end with the listed suffixes.

- Then call out some of the example words in the instruction note and ask students to identify their parts of speech.

2 **Practicing More Word Endings**

- Read the directions aloud, and explain the examples.

- Have students complete the activity.

- Call on students to share their answers.

ANSWER KEY

1. _n_ chapter
2. _n_ behavior
3. _v_ classify
4. _adj_ addicted
5. _n_ psychologist
6. _v_ concentrate
7. _adj_ computerized
8. _adj_ unlimited
9. _v_ visualize
10. _adj_ visual
11. _adj_ boring
12. _adj_ nuclear
13. _adj_ truthful
14. _n_ childhood
15. _adj_ bloody
16. _v_ simplify
17. _v_ organize
18. _n_ viewer
19. _n_ baby-sitter
20. _adj_ dissatisfied
21. _v_ personalize
22. _n_ relationship
23. _n_ emotionalism
24. _adj_ exciting
25. _n_ specialist
26. _adj_ shadowy
27. _v_ investigate
28. _v_ sadden
29. _adj_ natural
30. _n_ adulthood

- The aim of this activity is for students to internalize the concept of word families.

- Explain to students that you are going to say a list of words, and students will have five seconds to write down each word's part of speech. They will write *n* for nouns, *adj* for adjectives, and *adv* for adverbs.

- Read 5, 10, or 20 words, for example: " 1. exciting 2. viewer 3. . . . " Be sure to keep a record of the order in which you read the words.

- When you are finished, ask students to share the parts of speech they've written down. See how many people got all of the parts of speech correct.

Strategy

Understanding Word Families

- Have volunteers read the information in the Strategy box aloud.

- Write the examples from the box on the board and ask students if they can think of any other words that are in the same word family. Are any of the words in any single family the same part of speech?

3 **Choosing from Word Families**

- ❏ Read the directions aloud, and explain item 1.

- ❏ Have students complete the activity.

- ❏ Call on students to share their answers.

- ❏ Read and explain the directions below the activity aloud. Tell students that they can use this technique to increase their vocabulary.

ANSWER KEY

1. prefer, concentrate 2. addicted, visual
3. criticize, violence 4. behavior, childhood
5. Frequent, dissatisfied 6. envy, exciting 7. real, immoral 8. truth, personalities 9. psychological, suspenseful 10. strengthens, scary

Noun	Verb	Adjective
preference(s)	*prefer*	preferred preferable
concentration	*concentrate*	concentrated
addiction(s) addict	addict	*addicted*
vision(s)	*visualize*	*visual*
critic criticism	*criticize*	critical
violence	X	violent
behavior	*behave*	(well-)behaved
child children	X	childish childless
frequency	frequent	*frequent*
dissatisfaction	*dissatisfy*	dissatisfied

Noun	Verb	Adjective
envy	envy	envious
excitement	excite	exciting excited
reality	realize	real
immorality	X	immoral
truth	X	true truthful
personality personalities	personalize	personal
psychology	X	psychological
suspense	suspend	suspenseful suspended
strength	strengthen	strong
scare	scare	scary scared

4 Focusing on High-Frequency Words

❑ Read the directions aloud, and do the first item as a class.

❑ Have students complete the activity as you circulate and check their progress.

ANSWER KEY

1. programming 2. medicine 3. average
4. improve 5. elderly 6. hospitals 7. nursing
8. practice

5 Making Connections

Best Practice

Making Use of Academic Content

Activities such as this will enable students to better understand the ideas set forth in the reading passage. The task of doing an Internet search will allow students to develop the skills they need to conduct academic research.

❑ If you have access to a computer lab, conduct this activity in the lab so you can help students with their research. Complete the activity once as a class so students feel more comfortable doing it on their own. If you do not have access to a computer lab, assign this activity as homework.

❑ Have students work in pairs to share the information they found.

❑ Call on students to share their findings with the class.

FOCUSING ON COMPARISON AND CONTRAST IN READINGS

- Read and explain the information in the instruction note.

- Ask students to name two movies or two TV shows.

- Draw a Venn diagram on the board. Label the two circles with the names of the movies or shows, and label the overlapping part "Both."

- Ask students to name characteristics of the two movies or shows. Write the characteristics in a list. Prompt students to give characteristics like genres, lengths (of TV shows), actors, and so on.

- Place the characteristics in the correct places in the diagram. Explain that the overlapping part represents similarities between the movies or shows, and the circles represent differences. Note that you can also do this with two items in any category: books, people, pictures, and so on.

- Tell students to read the short personal stories

- Have students complete the activity independently.

- Call on students to share their answers.

 EXPANSION ACTIVITY

- The aim of this activity is for students to read a schedule and scan for specific information.

- Photocopy the Black Line Master, **Reading the TV Listings** (BLM 20) and distribute to students.

- Read the directions.

- Have students complete the activity.

- Call on students to share the information they found. If any students have written the same show in different categories, use the opportunity for a class discussion to determine what category the show belongs in. Note that the show may actually fit in more than one category.

ANSWER KEY

1. C 2. B 3. D 4. C 5. A

Self-Assessment Log

- ❏ Read the directions aloud, and have students check the strategies and vocabulary they learned in the chapter.

- ❏ Ask a volunteer to tell you where in the chapter information or an activity related to each strategy is located.

- ❏ Tell students to find definitions in the chapter for any words they did not check.

In this chapter, students will read about different methods for meeting romantic partners, such as arranged marriages, Internet dating, speed dating, and dance clubs. They will read the pros and cons of each method, and share their opinions about each. Students will read two selections from a fictional story called "Meeting the Perfect Mate," written by a woman who conducts interviews with a variety people about their ideas on the best way to meet the perfect mate. Students will have a chance to express their own ideas on the topic while practicing some essential academic strategies, such as predicting, understanding literal meanings and inferences, and recognizing the structure of written conversations.

Chapter Opener

- ❏ Direct students' attention to the photo and ask questions: *Who are these people? What are they doing?* (This photo is of a group of friends eating spaghetti.)

- ❏ Put students in small groups to discuss the questions in the **Connecting to the Topic** section.

- ❏ Read the quote by Ralph Waldo Emerson and ask students what they think it means.

- ❏ Put this sentence on the board: *I like to _____ with my friends*. Tell students to complete the sentence with an activity or two. Put students from different language groups in pairs (if possible) to discuss the sentence.

- ❏ Call on students to share their ideas with the class.

❝ The only way to have a friend is to be one. ❞

—Ralph Waldo Emerson
American author, poet, and philosopher (1803–1882)

Chapter Overview

Reading Skills and Strategies

Recognizing the structure of written conversations

Understanding left-out words and references

Reading for literal meaning and inferences

Critical Thinking Skills

Identifying pros and cons

Interpreting proverbs

Vocabulary Building

Understanding negative prefixes

Figuring out vocabulary from prefixes and suffixes

Language Skills

Discussing and comparing proverbs

Researching poems, quotes, and proverbs

Focus on Testing

Understanding inferences and points of view
  in readings

Vocabulary

Nouns	Verbs	Adjectives	Adverbs
feet*	arranged*	aggressive	enthusiastically
guy	interviewing	discouraged	fortunately*
inches*	match	optimistic	
match*	replied*	perfect*	
mates		popular*	
socks*		speedy*	
spouses		worried*	

*These words are among the 2,000 most-frequently used words in English.

Meeting the Perfect Mate

Content Notes

- Ralph Waldo Emerson is considered one of the most important American philosophers and writers. He was born in Boston, Massachusetts on May 25, 1803. Emerson associated very closely with Nathaniel Hawthorne and Henry David Thoreau. In fact, the land that Thoreau built his cabin on on Walden Pond belonged to Emerson.

- Emerson was at the center of the American Transcendental Movement, which was an important movement in literature and philosophy during the mid 19th century. The key principle of Transcendentalism was a "mystic unity of nature", which is discussed in his well-known essay, *Nature*.

Before You Read

1 Previewing the Topic

- ❏ Have students look at the illustrations. Check comprehension by asking a question: *What is happening in the pictures?*

- ❏ Have the students read the questions and write brief answers.

- ❏ Put students in small groups to practice asking and answering questions.

- ❏ Call on students to share their answers with the class.

2 Predicting

Best Practice

Activating Prior Knowledge

Activities such as this allow students to tap into their prior knowledge. Students learn more effectively when new information is meaningful to them, and working in groups to discuss and think about what they already know about a topic will allow them to actively link their prior knowledge to upcoming new information.

- ❏ Put students into small groups to discuss and write answers to the questions. Explain that it is OK to guess if they don't know the answers.

- ❏ Call on students to share their answers with the class.

- ❏ Tell students to look for the answers to the questions in the reading passage as they read.

3 Previewing Vocabulary

- ❏ Tell students to look at the list of vocabulary words, and repeat them after you read them aloud, or listen and repeat them as you play the tape or CD.

- ❏ Have them put a check mark (✓) next to the words they know.

Read

4 Reading an Article

- ❏ Have students read the passage silently within a time limit (15–20 minutes), or have them follow along silently as you play the tape or CD.

- ❏ Tell them to underline any words or phrases that are new or that they don't understand.

After You Read

RECOGNIZING THE STRUCTURE OF WRITTEN
CONVERSATIONS

- Read the information in the instruction note and explain as needed.

- To check comprehension, ask students to identify one sub-topic and one detail from the reading.

Best Practice

Organizing Information

Activities such as this one will teach students to organize information using a graphic organizer. This kind of chart allows students to better organize, assimilate, and recall information at a later date, a valuable study tool. In this case, students complete a chart for the main topics and supporting ideas of the reading passage.

5 **Recognizing the Structure of Written Conversations**

ANSWER KEY

Answers will vary in the Your Opinion column.

Interviewee	His or her method (= main idea)	Speaker's Pros	Speaker's Cons	Your Opinion
Usha	Arranged marriages	Husbands and wives may learn to love each other. Some very religious (orthodox) young people may marry this way today.	Spouses may meet for the first time on their wedding day.	
Bill	Meeting people in dance clubs, going to "speed dating" sessions	The club atmosphere is exciting, especially on weekends. You can dance, talk to people, or just listen to music. There are many attractive, active people there to meet. You meet a different potential date every six minutes. You list the names of the people you met that you want to see again.	People may drink, shout instead of talk, and become aggressive. If you're not a fast thinker or talker, there's not enough time to get to know people.	
Freddy	Finding friends in cyberspace	You can go online at home, at work or school, in cafés, and in other places. You can use your power notebook and video cell phone.	You don't know what is unreal or dangerous about people you meet on the Web.	
Julie	Meeting in health clubs or the gym	You can meet people with common interests.	If you're not really interested in exercise, there might be a problem.	

Main idea: There are many advantages and disadvantages to the various ways of meeting a mate.

Part 1

- ❏ Read the directions, and fill in a few of the boxes in the chart as a class.

- ❏ Have students complete the activity as you check their progress.

- ❏ Call on students to share their answers with the class.

REPRODUCIBLE   **EXPANSION ACTIVITY**

- ■ The aim of this activity is for students to interact with classmates and discuss the topic introduced in the reading passage.

- ■ Photocopy the Black Line Master, **Interview** (BLM 21), and distribute to students.

- ■ Read the directions.

- ■ Have students complete the activity.

- ■ Call on students to share the information they wrote in their charts.

6 **Understanding the Main Idea**

- ❏ Read the directions, and explain as necessary.

- ❏ Give students time to complete the activity as you check their work.

- ❏ Call on students to share their answers.

ANSWER KEY

Answers will vary. Possible answers:

There are (1) advantages and disadvantages to the various possible ways of meeting potential (2) mates. (3) A disadvantage of arranged marriages is that mates may not meet until their wedding day; even so, through the years they may learn to (4) love each other anyway. (5) At dance clubs, you can talk or just listen to (6) loud music; on the other hand, the people in such places tend to (7) drink too much, so they often act (8) aggressive. "Speed dating" is an organized way to meet potential friends, but it's probably most effective for (9) fast-talking, quick-thinking

people. Getting to know people in cyberspace is (10) convenient because computers and other electronic devices are (11) everywhere; however, (12) it is difficult to know what is unreal or unsafe about the people online. If you meet potential dates at a place where you have (13) something in common, like the gym, you can share your interest, but what happens if one person (14) loses interest in the activity?

Strategy

Understanding Left-Out Words and References

- ■ Read the information in the Strategy box, and explain as necessary.

- ■ To check comprehension, copy the first items from Activities 7 and 8, pages 193–194, on the board, and do them as a class.

7 **Providing Left-Out Words**

- ❏ Read the directions. Have students complete the activity as you monitor their progress.

- ❏ Call on students to share their answers with the class.

ANSWER KEY

Answers will vary. Possible answers:

1. match, how can you match 2. of arranged marriages 3. they were worried 4. meet a lot of women in dance clubs, to dance clubs

8 **Identifying References**

- ❏ Read the directions.

- ❏ Have students complete the activity as you monitor their progress.

- ❏ Call on students to share their answers with the class.

ANSWER KEY

1. seminar 2. an arranged marriage 3. My grandparents' children, my grandparents' children and their mates 4. Dance clubs seem great
5. in cyberspace 6. the healthy atmosphere in the gym is continuing into our relationship, wonderful
7. I hate to exercise

9 **Discussing the Reading**

Best Practice

Cultivating Critical Thinking

Activities such as this will help students practice analyzing information and determining their own opinions. In this activity, students consider the information from the reading and combine it with their own knowledge to discuss marriage and ways of meeting people.

❑ Put students into small groups to discuss answers to the questions. Ask them to take notes on their discussion.

❑ Call on students to share their answers with the class.

Meeting the Perfect Mate (continued)

Before You Read

1   **Previewing Vocabulary**

- ❑ Tell students look at the list of vocabulary words and repeat them after you, or listen and repeat them as you play the tape or CD.

- ❑ Have them put a check mark (✓) next to the words they know.

Strategy

Understanding Literal Meaning and Inferences

- ▪ Read the information in the Strategy box, and explain as necessary.

- ▪ To check comprehension, ask students to read lines 1–27 of "Meeting the Perfect Mate, Part 1" on page 188–189.

- ▪ Ask: *How does the writer respond to what Usha says?* Then ask: *What is the writer's opinion of arranged marriage? How can you tell?*

- ▪ Explain that you can infer the writer's opinion from what she says, even if she doesn't state her opinion directly.

Read

2   **Reading for Literal Meaning and Inferences**

- ❑ Read the directions, and explain as necessary.

- ❑ Have students read the passage silently within a time limit (10–15 minutes), or have students follow along silently as you play the tape or CD.

- ❑ Tell them to underline any words or phrases that are new or that they don't understand.

After You Read

3   **Identifying Literal Meaning and Inferences**

- ❑ Read the directions, and do the first three or four items as a class.

- ❑ Tell students to refer back to the Strategy box on page 195 as needed.

- ❑ Have students complete the activity as you monitor their progress.

- ❑ Call on students to share their answers.

ANSWER KEY

1. ✓   2. X   3. ✓   4. ✓   5. X   6. X   7. X   8. ✓   9. ✓
10. X   11. X   12. ✓   13. X   14. ✓   15. ✓   16. ✓

Strategy

Summarizing Stories by Identifying Pros and Cons

- ▪ Read the information in the Strategy box, and explain as necessary.

- ▪ To remind students what pros and cons are, have them look again at the chart in Activity 5 on page 191.

- ▪ Ask students to share pros and cons of the different dating methods in their own words.

4   **Summarizing Stories by Identifying Pros and Cons**

- ❑ Put students in groups of three, and read the directions aloud.

- ❑ Have each student complete three items and read their sentences aloud to the other members of their group.

- ❑ Call on students to read their sentences to the class.

ANSWER KEY

Answers will vary. Possible answers:

1. don't meet until their wedding day, but they can learn to love each other 2. there are many attractive people to meet, and you can dance, talk, or just listen to music / people drink, shout instead of talk, and become aggressive 3. really fast. You meet a new person every six minutes. / you are a fast talker and thinker / you aren't a fast talker and thinker 4. there are a lot of people online, and it's convenient / you don't know what is unreal or who is dangerous 5. there are people who have common interests / one person loses interest in the activity 6. you have a lot in common with the people you meet / aren't specific / find a match for you 7. you can watch someone's video and if you like them, you can meet them / a lot of people 8. it's easy to make small talk over the vegetables in the produce section 9. that arranged marriage might be a good idea after all

5 Discussing the Reading

❏ Put students into small groups to discuss answers to the questions. Ask them to take notes on their discussion.

❏ Call on students to share their answers with the class.

6 Talking It Over

❏ Read the directions aloud.

❏ Put students into small groups. Tell them to complete the activity on their own, then share their answers and discuss the questions with their group members.

❏ When students have finished talking with their group members, have students share their answers and reasons with the class.

ANSWER KEY

1. c 2. a 3. b 4. d 5. e 6. i 7. f 8. g 9. h 10. j

Scaffolding Instruction

Negative prefixes are introduced and practiced in this chapter in a step-by-step progression. First, students learn about the concept of negative prefixes and see some examples. Second, students complete an activity in which they identify these prefixes. Then, they complete an activity in which they fill in the correct prefixes on various words. This kind of scaffolded instruction allows students to thoroughly understand one part of a complex concept at a time.

Strategy

Identifying Negative Prefixes

- Read the information in the Strategy box, and explain as necessary.

- Ask students for examples of words that begin with the listed prefixes. *(disagree, disappear, illegal, illogical, impolite, immature, incorrect, inaccurate, nonrefundable, nontraditional, unfriendly, unhappy)*

1 Identifying Negative Prefixes

- ❑ Read the directions aloud, and explain if necessary.
- ❑ Have students complete the activity.
- ❑ Call on students to share their answers.

ANSWER KEY

1. N dis 2. X 3. N dis 4. N dis 5. N dis 6. X
7. N il 8. X 9. X 10. N im 11. N im 12. N im
13. N im 14. N im 15. N in 16. N in 17. in 18. X
19. X 20. N 21. X 22. N non 23. N non 24. N non
25. X 26. X 27. N un 28. N un 29. N un 30. N un

2 Filling in the Negative Prefix

- ❑ Read the directions aloud, and explain the examples.

- ❑ Have students complete the activity.
- ❑ Call on students to share their answers.

ANSWER KEY

1. dis 2. dis 3. un 4. un 5. in 6. in 7. un 8. un
9. il 10. im 11. un 12. im 13. im 14. non 15. un

3 Writing Opposites

- ❑ Read the directions aloud, and explain the first two examples.
- ❑ Have students complete the activity.
- ❑ Call on students to share their answers.
- ❑ Read and explain the directions below the activity aloud. Tell students that they can use this technique to increase their vocabulary.

ANSWER KEY

Answers will vary. Possible answers:

Some people looking for <u>possible</u> husbands and wives try <u>natural</u> methods. For instance, they might find it <u>easy</u> to make small talk with people that look <u>friendly</u> or <u>happy</u> in the produce section of the supermarket, where they are choosing <u>fresh</u> fruits and vegetables. Or they might have a conversation at a <u>fast</u>-food restaurant, where they <u>like</u> eating hamburgers, French fries, or other items with <u>low</u> nutritional value. In a <u>different</u> way, a computer service is <u>capable</u> of matching singles with <u>unmarried</u> people that are very much <u>like</u> them; men and women that get together in this <u>convenient</u> way often share many interests. A video-dating center may be <u>helpful</u> as well; meeting people on the Internet has benefits, but it can have <u>disadvantages</u> too. In any case, <u>few</u> ways of meeting people can be <u>successful</u> all the time.

EXPANSION ACTIVITY

- The aim of this activity is for students to internalize the concept of word families.

- Explain to students that you are going to say a list of words, and students will have five seconds to write down each word's opposite, using the prefixes they've learned.

- Read 5, 10, or 20 words from Activities 1–3, for example: "1. appearance, 2. convenient, 3. ..." Be sure to keep a record of the order in which you read the words.

- When you are finished, ask students to share the words they've written down.

4 **Figuring Out Vocabulary from Prefixes and Suffixes: Reading Personal Ads**

- ❏ Read the directions, and explain as necessary.

- ❏ Have students complete the activity with partners as you circulate and check their progress.

- ❏ When they are finished, have students share meanings of new or difficult words.

- ❏ Then have them match the men and women in the ads and explain the reasons for their matches.

ANSWER KEY

Answers will vary.

5 **Recognizing Words with Similar Meanings**

- ❏ Read the directions aloud, and do the first item as a class.

- ❏ Have students complete the activity as you circulate and check their progress.

ANSWER KEY

1. calm 2. slow 3. gal 4. quickly 5. daughter
6. arms 7. question 8. disrespect 9. pessimistic
10. unpopular

REPRODUCIBLE EXPANSION ACTIVITY

- The aim of this activity is for students to practice writing short descriptions.

- Photocopy the Black Line Master **Write a Personal Ad** (BLM 22), and distribute to students.

- Read the directions.

- Have students complete the activity.

6 **Focusing on High-Frequency Words**

- ❏ Read the directions aloud, and do the first item as a class.

- ❏ Have students complete the activity as you circulate and check their progress.

ANSWER KEY

1. international 2. arranged 3. match 4. tie
5. socks 6. grandparents 7. worried 8. bit 9. lot

7 **Making Connections**

Best Practice

Making Use of Academic Content

Activities such as this will enable students to better understand the ideas set forth in the reading passage. The task of doing an Internet search will allow students to develop the skills they need to conduct academic research.

❏ If you have access to a computer lab, conduct this activity in the lab so you can help students with their research. Complete the activity once as a class so students feel more comfortable doing the activity on their own. If you do not have access to a computer lab, assign this activity as homework.

❏ Have students work in pairs to share the information they found.

❏ Call on students to share their research with the class.

PRACTICING INFERENCES AND POINTS OF VIEW
IN READINGS

- Read and explain the information in the instruction note.

- Remind students that they practiced inferring meaning in Activity 3 on page 197.

- Read the directions, and explain as necessary.

- Have students complete the activity.

- Call on students to share their answers.

ANSWER KEY

1. B 2. C 3. D 4. D 5. C

EXPANSION ACTIVITY

- The aim of this activity is for students to internalize the definitions of the new vocabulary words.

- Photocopy the Black Line Master **Vocabulary Bingo** (BLM 23), and distribute to students.

- Read the directions. Write 20–25 vocabulary words from Part 3, Activities 1–3 on the board for students to choose from. Use both words with prefixes and words without. You will call out the opposites of these words, and students will mark the corresponding words on their cards. For example, if you say "advantage," they mark "disadvantage." Complete a partial Bingo card on the board.

- Model the activity by reading two or three words and marking their opposites on your card. Be sure to read the opposite of at least one word that is not on your card in order to show students that they don't mark anything if the word is not on their cards. Have students help you find the correct words on your Bingo card.

- Conduct the game. When a students shouts "Bingo!" check his or her answers.

- Optional: Give a prize to the winner.

- Note: Be sure to keep track of the words whose opposites you read.

Self-Assessment Log

- ❑ Read the directions aloud, and have students check the strategies and vocabulary they learned in the chapter.

- ❑ Ask a volunteer to tell you where in the chapter information or an activity related to each strategy is located.

- ❑ Tell students to find definitions in the chapter for any words they did not check.

Chapter 10

Sports

In this chapter, students will read about the similarities and differences between the ancient and modern Olympic games. They will also read two letters arguing for and against the continuation of competitive sports. The letters discuss such issues as the use of performance-enhancing drugs, the effects of corporate sponsorship on sports, scandal, patriotism, and pride. These topics will encourage students to consider and discuss their own views on competitive sports, fairness, nationalism, and sportsmanship.

Chapter Opener

❏ Direct students' attention to the photo and ask questions: *Who are these people? What are they doing?* (This photo is of the Women's Soccer 2003–World Cup–Canada vs. U.S.A.)

❏ Put students in small groups to discuss the questions in the **Connecting to the Topic** section.

❏ Read the quote and ask students how they think the Olympics might build a peaceful and better world.

❏ Put this sentence on the board: *My favorite sport to play is _____ because _____.* Tell students to complete the sentence by writing the name of their favorite sport and the reason it is their favorite. Put students from different language groups in pairs (if possible) to discuss the sentence.

❏ Call on students to share their ideas with the class.

❝ The goal of the Olympic movement is to contribute to building a peaceful and better world by educating youth through sport practiced without discrimination of any kind. ❞

—The Olympic Charter
paraphrased by the Amateur Athletic Foundation of Los Angeles, California

Chapter Overview

Reading Skills and Strategies

Recognizing reading structure: similarities and differences

Organizing supporting details using a Venn diagram

Critical Thinking Skills

Recognizing point of view

Distinguishing opinion from fact

Classifying supporting details

Comparing and contrasting the ancient and modern Olympics

Vocabulary Building

Understanding and working with prefixes, stems, and suffixes

Identifying antonyms

Language Skills

Researching and supporting points of view on competitive sports

Convincing others to understand a point of view

Focus on Testing

Taking notes and recognizing contrasts in reading passages

Vocabulary

Nouns	Verbs	Adjectives
achievement	boycotted	banned
competition*	canceled	competitive
conflict	competed*	extreme*
coordination	contributed	international*
demonstrations	corrupted	intolerable
fans*	decrease*	nondiscriminatory
opposition	disqualified	original*
organizations*	expand	profitable*
sports*	re-created	
	solve*	

*These words are among the 2,000 most-frequently used words in English.

The Ancient vs. the Modern Olympics

Before You Read

1 Previewing the Topic

- ❏ Have students look at the photos and pictures. Check comprehension by asking a question: *What is happening in the pictures?*

- ❏ Have the students read the questions and write brief answers.

- ❏ Put students in small groups to practice asking and answering questions.

- ❏ Call on students to share their answers with the class.

2 Predicting

Best Practice

Activating Prior Knowledge

Activities such as this allow students to tap into their prior knowledge. Students learn more effectively when new information is meaningful to them. Working in groups to discuss and think about what they already know about a topic will allow students to actively link their prior knowledge to upcoming new information.

- ❏ Put students into small groups to discuss and write answers to the questions. Explain that it is OK to guess if they don't know the answers.

- ❏ Call on students to share their answers with the class.

- ❏ Tell students to look for the answers to the questions in the reading passage as they read.

ANSWER KEY

Answers will vary.

3 Previewing Vocabulary

- ❏ Tell students to look at the list of vocabulary words and repeat them after you read them aloud, or listen and repeat them as you play the tape or CD.

- ❏ Have them put a check mark (✓) next to the words they know.

Read

Content Notes

- ■ Zeus is the king of the Greek gods. He is also god of the sky and of thunder. In Roman mythology, he is called Jupiter.

- ■ Hera is the Greek goddess of marriage, queen of the gods, and Zeus's wife. In Roman mythology, Zeus's wife was Juno.

- ■ A Spartan princess named Kyniska was the owner of the winning horses in the four-horse chariot race in 396 B.C.E. and 392 B.C.E. The women of Athens were very sheltered and received very little education. They had no say in Athenian politics. In contrast, Spartan women were very involved in the affairs of Sparta. They were educated, trained in sports, and encouraged to be as competitive as boys.

- ■ The ancient Olympic games took place for almost 1200 years. Theodocious I, one of the first Christian emperors of Rome, prohibted worship of pagan gods such as Zeus, so the games had to come to an end in 394 C.E. Theodocious I also ordered the temple of Zeus at Olympia to be burned down.

- ■ A Frenchman named Baron Pierre de Coubertin founded the modern Olympic Games. He first presented the idea of bringing back the Olympics in 1892. At first, he faced a lot of opposition. But after years of struggle, he finally convinced 13 countries to participate in the first modern Olympic

Games in Athens, Greece, in 1900. Only one medal was awarded for each event. The medals were made of silver.

■ In the ancient Olympic games, the Olympic flame symbolized the death and rebirth of Greek heroes. The flame was lit by the rays of the sun at Olympia and remained burning until the end of the Games. The tradition of the torch relay of the modern Olympics began in Berlin in 1936.

4 **Reading an Article**

❏ Have students read the passage silently within a time limit (15 minutes), or have students follow along silently as you play the tape or CD.

❏ Tell them to underline any words or phrases that are new or that they don't understand.

After You Read

5 **Recognizing Reading Structure: Similarities and Differences**

❏ Read the directions, and go over the first two items.

❏ Have students complete the activity as you check their progress.

❏ Call on students to share their answers with the class.

ANSWER KEY

1. A 2. both 3. A 4. A 5. M 6. A

EXPANSION ACTIVITY

REPRODUCIBLE

■ The aim of this activity is for students to practice making comparisons.

■ Photocopy the Black Line Master, **Comparing Sports** (BLM 24), and distribute to students.

■ Read the directions.

■ Have students complete the activity.

■ Call on students to share the information they wrote in their Venn diagrams.

6 **Understanding the Main Idea**

❏ Read the directions and explain as necessary.

❏ Give students time to complete the activity as you check their work.

❏ Call on students to share their answers.

ANSWER KEY

c: Ways that the ancient and modern Olympics are similar: every four years, opening ceremony, judges' promise of fairness, spectators, prizes for winning athletes

Strategy

Using a Venn Diagram to Organize Supporting Details

■ Read the information in the Strategy box and explain as needed.

■ Tell students to read the phrases about the Olympics before each Venn diagram.

■ Ask them to decide whether each phrase is a detail about the ancient and/or modern Olympics, then write the letter in the correct place in the Venn diagrams.

Best Practice

Organizing Information

Activities such as this one will teach students to organize information using a graphic organizer. This kind of chart allows students to better organize, assimilate, and recall information at a later date, a valuable study tool. In this case, students complete diagrams comparing and contrasting information from two articles.

ANSWER KEY

The Olympic Events

Ancient Olympic Games: B. held at the sanctuary of Zeus on Mt. Olympus near Athens, Greece E. include sacrifices in honor of Zeus as well as feasts H. include other events = four-horse chariot race, extreme wrestling and boxing J. offer prizes = olive tree wreaths

Both: A. take place every four summers D. begin with promises of fairness by athletes and judges G. include some sports competitions = footraces, the pentathlon, equestrian events

Modern Olympic Games: C. held in various world cities F. start with the lighting of the Olympic Cauldron as part of the opening ceremony I. include other events = aquatics, cycling, soccer, basketball, volleyball, gymnastics K. offer prizes = gold, silver, and bronze medals for 1st, 2nd, 3rd places

Women in the Olympic Games

Ancient Olympic Games: O. married women in sanctuary of Zeus were killed (thrown off a cliff) M. unmarried women only = in footraces and audience

Both: L. more men than women participants

Modern Olympic Games: N. women athletes in many sports P. small number of women in Olympic organizations is an issue

The Politics of the Olympics

Ancient Olympic Games: R. three-month peace agreement among rival city-states to protect travelers to and from the Games

Both: Q. spirit of the Games = contribution to peace

Modern Olympic Games: S. Olympics canceled because of hostilities during two World Wars T. sometimes political boycotts of the Olympics and terrorist attacks during them

7 **Discussing the Reading**

Best Practice

Cultivating Critical Thinking

Activities such as this will help students practice analyzing information and determining their own opinions. In this activity, students consider the information from the reading and combine it with their own knowledge to discuss the Olympics.

❑ Put students into small groups to discuss answers to the questions. Ask them to take notes on their discussion.

❑ Call on students to share their answers with the class.

Issues in Competitive Sports

Before You Read

1 Previewing Vocabulary

- ❑ Tell students look at the list of vocabulary words and repeat them after you, or listen and repeat them as you play the tape or CD.

- ❑ Have them put a check mark (✓) next to the words they know.

Read

2 Recognizing Point of View

- ❑ Read the directions and explain as necessary.

- ❑ Have students read the passage silently within a time limit (10–15 minutes), or have students follow along silently as you play the tape or CD.

- ❑ Tell them to underline any words or phrases that are new or that they don't understand. Make sure students complete the titles of the reading passages.

ANSWER KEY

Part 1: The World Should <u>Stop</u> Sports Competition

Part 2: The World Should <u>Promote</u> Sports Competition

After You Read

Strategy

Distinguishing Opinion from Fact

- ▪ Read the information in the Strategy box, and explain as necessary.

- ▪ To check comprehension, have students find one opinion and one fact in the reading passage.

3 Identifying Opinions and Facts

- ❑ Read the directions, and do the first item as a class.

- ❑ Have students complete the activity as you monitor their progress.

- ❑ Call on students to share their answers.

ANSWER KEY

1. F 2. O 3. F 4. F 5. O 6. F 7. O 8. O

Strategy

Summarizing Opinions

- ▪ Read the information in the Strategy box, and explain as necessary.

- ▪ To check comprehension, ask students to explain the bullet points in their own words. Clarify as necessary.

- ▪ Review the connecting words presented in Chapter 7 if needed.

4 Summarizing Opinions

- ❑ Put students in even-numbered groups (4 or 6), and read the directions aloud.

- ❑ Have each group break into two smaller groups. Have the smaller groups choose one of the two articles to summarize.

- ❑ Have groups write their summaries, then work together to revise and clarify them.

- ❑ Have the groups choose which of their two summaries is most convincing.

- ❑ Call on groups to share their summaries with the class.

5   Discussing the Reading

Best Practice

Interacting with Others

These types of collaborative activities help students get a better understanding of the ideas in the reading passage through interacting with other students. They can clarify their ideas and reinforce knowledge with the assistance of their group members.

❑ Put students into small groups to discuss answers to the questions. Ask them to take notes on their discussion.

❑ Call on students to share their answers with the class.

6   Talking It Over

❑ Read the directions aloud.

❑ Tell students to complete the matching part of the activity on their own.

❑ When students have finished the matching part of the activity, put them into groups of four, and assign one of the five issues to each group.

❑ Have groups break into pairs to prepare arguments on opposing sides of the issue they were assigned.

❑ Have pairs discuss their side and prepare their arguments.

❑ When students have finished talking with their partners, have each group of four present their opposing arguments to the class.

❑ Have the class vote for the best-argued presentation.

ANSWER KEY

Part 1: 1. c   2. e   3. a   4. b   5. d

REPRODUCIBLE   **EXPANSION ACTIVITY**

■ The aim of this activity is for students to internalize the concept of contrasting opinions.

■ Photocopy the Black Line Master **Contrasting Opinions: Olympic Sports** (BLM 25), and distribute to students.

■ Read the directions.

■ Give students 15–25 minutes to complete the activity as you check their progress.

■ Have groups present their opposing opinions and points to the class.

■ Have the class vote on a side based only on what the groups have said, and not on their opinions about the issue. Have students explain why they chose one side over the other.

Best Practice

Scaffolding Instruction

Prefixes and suffixes are introduced and practiced in this book in a step-by-step progression. Suffixes were introduced and practiced in Chapters 7 and 8, and negative prefixes were introduced and practiced in Chapter 9. In this chapter, students continue to work with both prefixes and suffixes. This kind of scaffolded instruction allows students to thoroughly understand one part of a complex concept at a time.

Strategy

Understanding Prefixes

- Read the information, and explain as necessary.

- Ask students to find the following words in the reading passages: *corrupted, conflict, coordination, competition, competing, exceptions, international, re-created, promote, cooperative, prevent, protect, expand, decrease*.

1   Understanding Prefixes: Matching

- ❑ Read the directions aloud, and explain as necessary.

- ❑ Have students complete the activity.

- ❑ Call on students to share their answers.

- ❑ Have students look at the chart below the activity and call out words that begin with the prefixes listed.

ANSWER KEY

1. c 2. j 3. e 4. i 5. h 6. d 7. f 8. g 9. a 10. b

REVIEWING PREFIXES

- Read the information in the instruction note and explain as needed.

- Remind students that they can use prefixes as clues to unfamiliar words.

- Tell them that they can also use their dictionaries if they need to.

2   Understanding Prefixes: Fill in the Blank

- ❑ Read the directions aloud, and explain the examples.

- ❑ Have students complete the activity.

- ❑ Call on students to share their answers.

ANSWER KEY

1. consists, recreation, competition, compete, achieve 2. resembling, objects, events, evolved, included, connected, universally, different, addition, introduced, relays 3. production, increased, enabled, observe, professional, advent

Strategy

Understanding Prefixes, Stems, and Suffixes

- Read the information, and explain as necessary.

- Ask students for examples of prefixes and suffixes. If they have trouble remembering suffixes, have them turn to Chapter 7, page 151, or Chapter 8, page 176.

3   Practicing Prefixes, Stems, and Suffixes

- ❑ Read the directions aloud, and explain the first two blanks.

- ❑ Have students complete the activity.

- ❑ Call on students to share their answers.

ANSWER KEY

1. describes, recreation, professional, individual, transportation, environmentally, invention, development, commonly 2. concept, different, renowned, event, involves, promote, constructed, prevent, prevails

EXPANSION ACTIVITY

- The aim of this activity is for students to internalize the concept of prefixes.

- Explain to students that you are going to name prefixes, and students will have one minute to write down as many words beginning with that prefix as possible.

- Read 5–10 prefixes from Chapters 9 and 10, and give students time to write words. Be sure to keep a record of the prefixes you read.

- When you are finished, ask students to share the words they've written down.

4 Identifying Antonyms

- ❑ Read the directions aloud, and do the first two items as a class.

- ❑ Have students complete the activity as you circulate and check their progress.

ANSWER KEY

1. f 2. l 3. c 4. i 5. a 6. e 7. j 8. b 9. h 10. k
11. d 12. g

5 Focusing on High-Frequency Words

- ❑ Read the directions aloud, and do the first item as a class.

- ❑ Have students complete the activity as you circulate and check their progress.

ANSWER KEY

1. female 2. fencing 3. track 4. competed
5. original 6. international 7. sports
8. organizations

6 Making Connections

Best Practice

Making Use of Academic Content

Activities such as this will enable students to better understand the ideas set forth in the reading passages about sports. The task of doing an Internet search will allow students to develop the skills they need to conduct academic research.

- ❑ If you have access to a computer lab, conduct this activity in the lab so you can help students with their research. Complete the activity once as a class so students feel more comfortable doing the activity on their own. If you do not have access to a computer lab, assign this activity as homework.

- ❑ Have students work in pairs to share the information they found.

- ❑ Call on students to share their research with the class.

TOEFL® IBT

PRACTICING TAKING NOTES ABOUT CONTRASTS

- Read and explain the information in the instruction note on Taking Notes and Recognizing Contrasts in Reading Passages.

- To demonstrate the note-taking technique described, draw a vertical line on the board to make two columns and label one column "For" and the other "Against." Ask students to look at the reading that begins on page 219. Ask volunteers to find and call out contrasting points in the reading as you record them in note form on the board. Be sure to place parallel contrasting ideas next to each other.

- Read the directions and explain as necessary.

- Have students complete the activity.

- Call on students to share their answers.

ANSWER KEY

1. D 2. B 3. B 4. A 5. D 6. C

 EXPANSION ACTIVITY

- The aim of this activity is for students to practice doing Internet research and to practice scanning for information.

- Photocopy the Black Line Master **Internet Search: Olympic Athletes** (BLM 26), and distribute to students.

- Read the directions.

- Have students complete the activity.

- Call on students to share the information they found.

Self-Assessment Log

- Read the directions aloud, and have students check the strategies and vocabulary they learned in the chapter.

- Ask a volunteer to tell you where in the chapter information or an activity related to each strategy is located.

- Tell students to find definitions in the chapter for any words they did not check.

BLM 1

Name _____ Date _____

What do we have in common?

Directions: Work with a partner. Ask each other the questions on page 13, Activity 4, item 1. You can ask additional questions if you like. Take notes on your answers and your partner's answers. Then complete the Venn diagram below. Put information about yourself in one circle, information about your partner in the other circle, and things that are true about both of you in the middle.

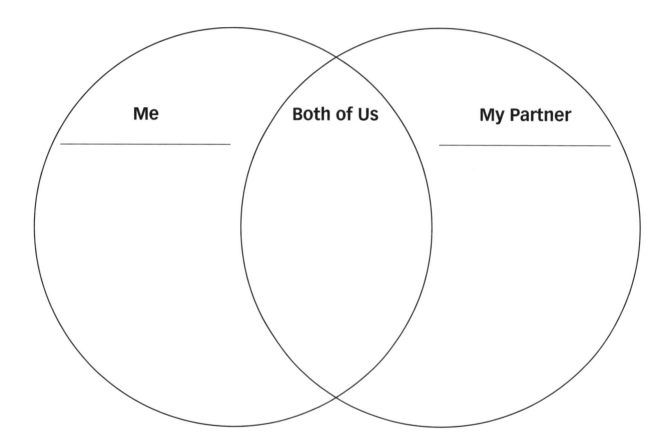

Name _____   Date _____

Making Comparisons: Internet Search

Directions: As you do Activity 5 on page 18, look at the information you found about offerings, requirements, and what you like. Then think about four or five things that are important to you in choosing a college or university (sometimes called a *school*). Write these "important questions" on the lines. Then research two colleges or universities and write the answers to these important questions on the T-chart below. When you have completed the T-chart, decide which school you would like better.

Important Questions:

Examples: Does the school have a good English language program?

Does the school offer _____ as a major?

Does the school have a soccer team?

How many students attend the school?

1. _____

2. _____

3. _____

4. _____

5. _____

School A: _____ | **School B:** _____

 **BLM 3**

Name _____ Date _____

Vocabulary Bingo

Directions: Write one vocabulary word in each square of the Bingo card below. Your teacher will read some definitions. When you hear the definition of a word on your card, draw an "X" on the word. The first person to draw a straight line of X's and shout "Bingo!" is the winner.

Name _____   Date _____

Solutions for Global Warming

Directions: Work in a small group. Paragraph D of the article "Global Climate Changes" on page 31 says that people are probably the main cause of extreme weather and changes to the global climate. Because of things people are doing, we are putting more and more gases like carbon dioxide into the air. Complete the following task with your group:

- ❏ Complete the cluster diagram by writing down things that people are doing to cause the problem
- ❏ Brainstorm ways to solve the problem.

Things we are doing to cause the problem:

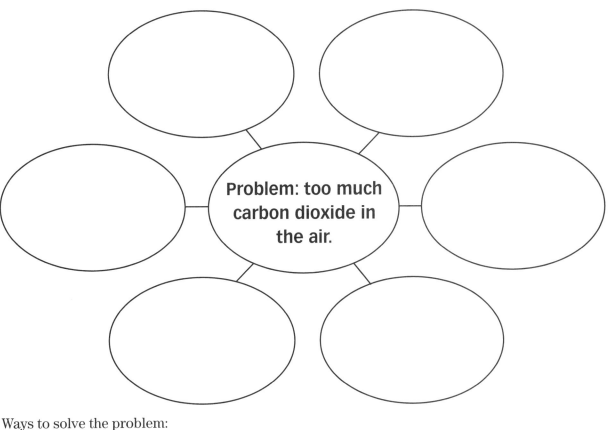

Problem: too much carbon dioxide in the air.

Ways to solve the problem:

_____

_____

_____

_____

Name _____ Date _____

Weather Forecast

Directions: Go to a weather website such as www.weather.com. Look up the 5-day forecast for a city that you are interested in visiting. Fill in the 5-day chart below with the name of each day, each day's high and low temperature, and a "picture" of the weather for the day.

City: _____

Day: _____	Day: _____	Day: _____	Day: _____	Day: _____
High: _____	High: _____	High: _____	High: _____	High: _____
Low: _____	Low: _____	Low: _____	Low: _____	Low: _____
Weather:	Weather:	Weather:	Weather:	Weather:

Name _____   Date _____

A Food Diary

Directions: For one week, keep track of all the food you eat and the beverages you drink. Write the days of the week in the first column. Write the foods and beverages and where they came from in the middle column. For example, did you buy the food at a fast food restaurant? Did you make it at home? Then think about why you chose the things you ate and drank. Write the reasons for your diet decisions in the third column.

Day of the Week	Foods and Beverages/ Where They Came From	Reasons I Chose These Foods and Beverages

Name _____   Date _____

Finding Food Facts

Directions: Go to a search engine and type in keywords like "calorie counts" and "nutritional information." You can also use websites such as www.fatcalories.com or www.foodfacts.info. Find a website that provides nutritional information about foods. Look up information for five food items from five different fast-food restaurants. For each food item, write down the number of calories, the number of fat calories, and the address of the website you used.

Food Item	Fast-Food Restaurant	Total Calories	Fat Calories	Website Address
1. *hamburger*				
2.				
3.				
4.				
5.				

Name _____   Date _____

Asking for and Giving Directions

Directions: With your class, brainstorm a list of places near campus that you and your classmates like to go; for example, restaurants, coffee shops, bookstores, and so on. Then complete the following steps:

❏ Choose one of the places from your class's list and write step-by-step directions from your school to that place.

❏ Draw a map from your school to the place in the space below.

❏ Work with a partner to ask for and give directions to the place you chose.

❏ As you listen to your partner give you directions, draw a map in the space at the bottom of the page. Then compare your map to the map your partner drew. Is it the same?

Map to my target place: _____

Map to my partner's target place: _____

BLM 9

Name _____   Date _____

Real or Not Real?

Directions: Some of the laws below are real and some are not. Put an "R" next to the laws that you think are real and "NR" next to the ones that you think are made up.

_____ **1.** In Baltimore, Maryland, it is illegal to take a lion to the movies.

_____ **2.** In Topeka, Kansas, it is illegal for restaurant servers to serve wine in teacups.

_____ **3.** In Las Vegas, Nevada, it is illegal to drink alcohol while playing cards.

_____ **4.** In Lincoln, Nebraska, it is illegal to wear boots inside a hospital.

_____ **5.** In New York State, it is illegal to smoke within 100 feet of the entrance to a public building.

_____ **6.** In Devon, Connecticut, it is illegal to walk backwards after sunset.

_____ **7.** In Seattle, Washington, it is illegal to bring an umbrella into a gas station.

_____ **8.** In Oklahoma, it is illegal to make "ugly faces" at dogs.

_____ **9.** In Pacific Grove, California, it is illegal to harm butterflies.

_____ **10.** In Joliet, Illinois, it is illegal to mispronounce the name Joliet.

Information found on:
http://www.geocities.com/CollegePark/Library/5663/laws.html
http://tjshome.com/dumblaws.php.

Name _____   Date _____

Making New Laws

Directions: Work in a small group to brainstorm ideas for four new laws at your school. Write the new laws in the first column, then work alone to complete the rest of the chart.

New Laws for Your School	Reasons for These Laws	Is it a good law for your home? Why or Why Not?
1.		
2.		
3.		
4.		

Name _____   Date _____

Comparing Families

Directions: Work with a partner. Describe your families to each other. Describe either your current family living situation or your living situation when you were growing up. Do not describe your situation as a student living away from home to attend school. Consider these kinds of questions as you describe your family: Do you have a single-parent family? A two-paycheck family? A blended family? Do you live in a nuclear family structure? An extended family? Are there any children in your family? How many? Complete the following tasks with your partner:

❑ Complete the T-chart by writing down descriptions of your families.

❑ Complete the Venn diagram by putting the descriptions in the correct sections.

My Family	My Partner's Family

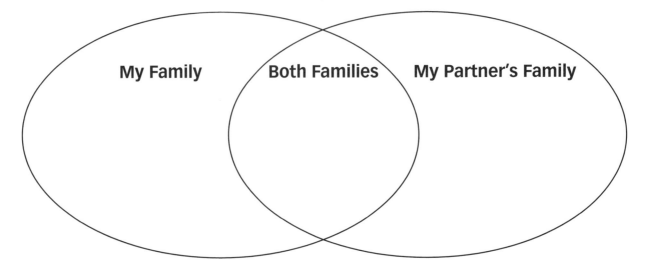

Name _____   Date _____

Traditional Roles: Pros and Cons

Directions: In American society, it is considered *traditional* that women stay home and take care of the house and the children while men work outside the home and earn all the money for the family. Work in small groups. Brainstorm some pros (positive things) and cons (negative things) about traditional gender roles and list them in the chart below.

Pros of Traditional Gender Roles	Cons of Traditional Gender Roles

Name _____ Date _____

Vocabulary Bingo

Directions: Write one vocabulary word in each square of the Bingo card below. Your teacher will read some definitions. When you hear the definition of a word on your card, draw an "X" on the word. The first person to draw four Xs in a straight line and shouts "Bingo!" is the winner.

BLM 14

Name _____ Date _____

Achievements of My Culture

Directions: Go to a search engine on the Internet. Find information about four examples of art, architecture, music, literature, or technological or scientific discoveries from any time period in your culture. Use the information to complete the chart below.

What is it?	When was it built, written, discovered, etc.?	How or why is it important to your culture?
1.		
2.		
3.		
4.		

Name _____ Date _____

What Makes a Culture?

Directions: What kinds of things make up a culture? For example, art, architecture, and literature help to define a culture. But what other things are important to a culture? Work in a small group, and brainstorm a list of things that help to define a culture. Then have a discussion with your group to decide what your group thinks are the five most important things that define a culture. List them from 1 to 5, with 1 being the most important.

You and your group members might disagree with each other's opinions. Practice disagreeing politely.

Brainstorm:

art

architecture

literature

_____   _____   _____

_____   _____   _____

_____   _____   _____

_____   _____   _____

_____   _____   _____

_____   _____   _____

Five Most Important Things:

1. _____

2. _____

3. _____

4. _____

5. _____

Name _____ Date _____

Comparing Lifestyles and Researching Life Expectancy

Part 1: First, compare your lifestyle (diet, exercise, stress levels, etc.) with the lifestyle of one of the groups you read about in the article "The Secrets of a Very Long Life." Complete the Venn diagram below and write a short paragraph summarizing the information in your Venn diagram.

Part 2: Second, go to a search engine. Find a website that allows you to calculate your own, or someone else's, life expectancy. Use keywords like "life expectancy calculator" or "life expectancy test." You will be asked to answer questions about lifestyle, diet, exercise, and other habits. When you're finished, complete the sentence at the bottom of this page.

Part 1

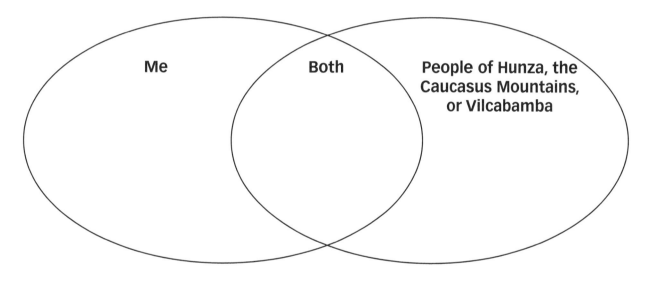

Me   Both   People of Hunza, the Caucasus Mountains, or Vilcabamba

Summary:

_____

_____

_____

_____

_____

_____

Part 2

My life expectancy is _____ years.

Name _____   Date _____

Internet Search: Diseases and Cures

Directions: Use a search engine to search the Internet. Research a disease or illness. Find the symptoms (problems that show you have a particular disease or illness), causes, and, cures or treatments (things that people with the disease can do to feel better) of the disease or illness. Use the name of the disease and the words "symptoms" and "cures" as keywords. Complete the chart below with the information you find. Include the sources (websites) you used.

Name of the Disease or Illness: _____   **Sources:** _____   _____   _____   _____
Symptoms:
Causes:
Cures/Treatments:

BLM 18

Name _____ Date _____

Find Your Match

Teacher: Cut out these slips and distribute to students.

root: *differ* Word: _____ Part of Speech: _____ Classmate's Name: _____	root: *ignore* Word: _____ Part of Speech: _____ Classmate's Name: _____	root: *agree* Word: _____ Part of Speech: _____ Classmate's Name: _____
root: *require* Word: _____ Part of Speech: _____ Classmate's Name: _____	root: *disappear* Word: _____ Part of Speech: _____ Classmate's Name: _____	root: *prevent* Word: _____ Part of Speech: _____ Classmate's Name: _____
root: *believ-* Word: _____ Part of Speech: _____ Classmate's Name: _____	root: *resid-* Word: _____ Part of Speech: _____ Classmate's Name: _____	root: *magnific-* Word: _____ Part of Speech: _____ Classmate's Name: _____
root: *act* Word: _____ Part of Speech: _____ Classmate's Name: _____	root: *avail* Word: _____ Part of Speech: _____ Classmate's Name: _____	root: *product* Word: _____ Part of Speech: _____ Classmate's Name: _____
root: *happi* Word: _____ Part of Speech: _____ Classmate's Name: _____	root: *change* Word: _____ Part of Speech: _____ Classmate's Name: _____	root: *amuse* Word: _____ Part of Speech: _____ Classmate's Name: _____
suffix: *ent* Word: _____ Part of Speech: _____ Classmate's Name: _____	suffix: *ence* Word: _____ Part of Speech: _____ Classmate's Name: _____	suffix: *able* Word: _____ Part of Speech: _____ Classmate's Name: _____
suffix: *ment* Word: _____ Part of Speech: _____ Classmate's Name: _____	suffix: *ion* Word: _____ Part of Speech: _____ Classmate's Name: _____	suffix: *ive* Word: _____ Part of Speech: _____ Classmate's Name: _____
suffix: *ant* Word: _____ Part of Speech: _____ Classmate's Name: _____	suffix: *ness* Word: _____ Part of Speech: _____ Classmate's Name: _____	suffix: *ance* Word: _____ Part of Speech: _____ Classmate's Name: _____

 **BLM 19**

Name _____ Date _____

Visual Media Journal

Directions: Keep track of how much visual media you are exposed to for two days in a row. For the next two days, write down how much time you spend watching TV, seeing movies, and surfing the Internet. Also, keep track of what kinds of shows you watch and what kind of movies you see. Then answer the question below the chart.

	TV: Hours and types of shows	Movies: Hours and types of movies	Internet: Hours
Day 1			
Day 2			

Do you think you watch too much TV, see too many movies, spend too much time surfing the Internet? Why or why not?

_____

_____

_____

_____

_____

Name _____   Date _____

Reading the TV Listings

Directions: Find a website or newspaper that provides local TV listings. Look through the listings for one day from 8:00 PM to 10:00 PM. How many of each kind of show can you find? Complete the chart below with show titles.

	Show Titles
Adventure or Action	
Crime or Mystery	
Authentic History	
Serious Drama	
Suspense or Horror	
Science Fiction or Fantasy	
Comedy	
Animated Cartoon	
Musical	
Biography or People's Personal Experiences	
Reality TV	
News	

Name _____ Date _____

Interview

Directions: Interview five classmates. Ask them what methods they know for meeting a possible mate or new friends. Complete the chart.

Classmate's Name	His or Her Method	Pros of the Method	Cons of the Method	Will you try the method? Why or why not?
1.				
2.				
3.				
4.				
5.				

Name _____ Date _____

Write a Personal Ad

Directions: Write a personal ad. First, complete the chart. Then, use the information in your chart to write a short paragraph describing yourself and your ideal partner.

Questions	Answers
1. Are you single, married, divorced, or widowed?	
2. How old are you?	
3. What do you look like?	
4. What are your hobbies and interests? What do you like to do?	
5. Are you looking for a man or woman? Are you looking for friendship or a romantic relationship?	
6. How old is your ideal partner?	
7. Is appearance important to you? What does your ideal partner look like?	
8. Is your partner's religion important to you? Explain.	
9. What do you NOT want in a partner?	

PERSONALS _____ **SEEKING** _____

_____

_____

_____

_____

_____

_____

_____

_____

Name _____   Date _____

Vocabulary Bingo

Directions: Write one vocabulary word in each square of the Bingo card below. Your teacher will read some words. When you hear the opposite of a word on your card, draw an "X" on the word. The first person to draw a straight line of X's and shout "Bingo!" is the winner.

Name _____   Date _____

Comparing Sports

Directions: Work with a partner to compare two sports. Choose a sport from the choices below, or choose two other sports to compare. First, brainstorm a list of characteristics (descriptions) for each of the sports you chose. Then write each characteristic in the correct place in the Venn diagram.

basketball and soccer	soccer and hockey
football and soccer	volleyball and basketball
swimming and running	shooting (gun) and archery (bow and arrow)
figure skating and dancing	skiing and snowboarding
figure skating and gymnastics	race car driving and horse racing

Characteristics

Sport: _____	Sport: _____

Sport: _____   **Both**   Sport: _____

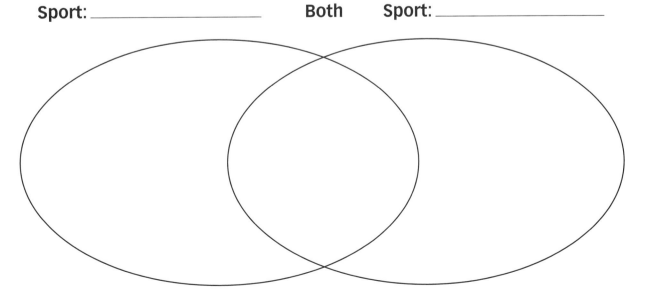

Name _____   Date _____

Contrasting Opinions: Olympic Sports

Directions: Should the sports below be included in the Olympics? Why or why not? Work in a group of four or six to choose a sport. You can choose one of the sports below or your group can decide on a different sport. Note that some of the choices below are currently Olympic sports. Break your group into two teams. Each team chooses one side (*for* or *against*) and lists reasons on one side of the chart below why the sport should or should not be included in the Olympics.

When you are finished, your group will present opposing points of view to the class. The class will vote on which team had the most convincing arguments.

Sports		
❏ snowboarding ❏ surfing ❏ basketball ❏ volleyball ❏ boxing	❏ American football ❏ martial arts (for example: karate, tae kwon do, capoeira) ❏ ballroom dancing	❏ baseball ❏ synchronized swimming ❏ figure skating ❏ equestrian sports ❏ curling

Sport: _____	
For	**Against**

BLM 26

Name _____   Date _____

Internet Search: Olympic Athletes

Directions: Go to the Internet and use a search engine to find a website about the Olympics. For each of the sports listed below, find one athlete who competed during the last summer or winter Olympic games. Write the athlete's name and country.

Sport	Name	Country
1. downhill skiing		
2. figure skating		
3. snowboarding		
4. biathlon		
5. swimming		
6. table tennis		
7. gymnastics		
8. cycling		
9. tae kwon do		
10. modern pentathlon		

Chapter 1 Test

International Students: The Challenge of a New Language

Section I Reading Comprehension Read the passage. Then answer the questions that follow. **(5 points each)**

Life Abroad Can Be Challenging

A   There are many great advantages to being an international student. The meaning of *advantage* is "something that is helpful to you in some way." International students can learn new languages, study subjects that aren't available in their own countries, and find out about different cultures. But life abroad can be challenging, too. For example, many students living abroad can't speak the language of their new country very well when they first arrive. Some students can have trouble finding an apartment, shopping for food, or understanding the public transportation system in a new city. Students can also have difficulty registering for classes or understanding their teachers. It can be very hard for foreign students to meet new friends, too. But there are several things international students can do to make their lives a little easier.

Tip #1: Visit the International Student Office

B   First of all, most colleges and universities have an International Student Office. Foreign students can use the office's services to find apartments or rooms to rent. These offices usually have information about language tutors and campus facilities, too. Also, they are available to help students with anything—including things like bus schedules and food shopping.

Tip #2: Talk to Teachers

C   It can be very difficult for foreign students to understand what's happening in their classes. Talking to teachers can be helpful. In many countries, teachers are happy to answer questions after class or during office hours. Some teachers allow students to record their lectures. That way, a student can listen to a lecture as many times as he or she wants to. And if a student has trouble understanding what a teacher said during part of a lecture, the student can play that part back to the teacher and ask for clarification.

Tip #3: Practice Speaking

D   International students can also find many ways to practice speaking their new language. For example, they can attend social events. People at parties or sporting events are usually more willing to talk with someone new. They can join student clubs, too. That way, they can not only practice their new language, they can also make new friends.

1. What is the main idea of this article?

(A) Foreign students can join student clubs to practice speaking their new language.

(B) There are a lot of things foreign students can do to make their lives less challenging.

(C) Life abroad can be challenging for an international student.

(D) The International Student Office offers important services for foreign students.

2. At an International Student Office, students can _____

(A) get help finding an apartment or joining a club.

(B) take a bus to a grocery store.

(C) find a language tutor and make new friends.

(D) find out about campus resources.

3. According to the article, in some classes, students can _____

(A) record their teachers' lectures.

(B) talk to teachers during class.

(C) make new friends.

(D) practice speaking their new language.

4. Joining student clubs can be a great way to _____

(A) make new friends and attend campus events.

(B) practice speaking and meet new people.

(C) meet new people and get help with homework.

(D) attend sporting events and parties on campus.

5. To ask for information about the library, an international student can _____

(A) join a student group or club.

(B) attend a campus event.

(C) visit a teacher after class or during office hours.

(D) go to the International Student Office.

Section II Strategy Four of the items below are main ideas from the article "International Students: The Challenge of a New Language." One of them is a supporting detail. Match each main idea with the related paragraph. Write the letter of the paragraph on the line. Write "SD" next to the item that is a supporting detail. **(5 points each)**

1. _____ International students can talk to their teachers if they are having problems understanding their

classes.

2. _____ Life abroad can be both helpful to international students and difficult for them. But there are a

lot of things they can do to get help.

3. _____ Students can go to the International Student Office for help with many different problems.

4. _____ There are a lot of ways to practice speaking a new language.

5. _____ Some teachers allow students to record their lectures so they can listen to them as many times

as they want to.

Section III New Words Match each vocabulary word on the left with the correct definition on the right. **(3 points each)**

1. _____ relaxed   **a.** necessary courses

2. _____ facilities   **b.** a teacher

3. _____ requirements   **c.** to go to (a school)

4. _____ a quiz   **d.** calm

5. _____ similar   **e.** to finish or end something

6. _____ an instructor   **f.** abilities

7. _____ attend   **g.** the buildings and equipment of a school, college, or university

8. _____ complete   **h.** a method or way

9. _____ skills   **i.** just about the same

10. _____ a style   **j.** a test

Section IV Vocabulary and Language Learning Skills In each group of words, find the three words with the same or similar meanings. Which word doesn't belong? Cross it out. **(4 points each)**

1.	university	college	job	school
2.	method	view	idea	opinion
3.	certificate	degree	proof of completion	exam
4.	tuition	scholarship	fee	charge
5.	class	homework	seminar	course

TOTAL _____ /100 pts.

Name _____ Date _____ Score _____

Chapter 2 Test

Rain Forests and the Earth's Climate

Section I Reading Comprehension Read the passage. Then answer the questions that follow.
(5 points each)

The Importance of Rain Forests

A   Rain forests cover only about six percent of the earth's surface, but they are very important to the earth. What is a rain forest? It is an area of land that gets a lot of rainfall and is mostly covered by tall, old trees. Some rain forests get up to 33 feet (10 meters) of rain each year. Some of their trees are thousands of years old. Most of the world's rain forests are in Africa, Asia, Australia, Central America, and South America. More than half of the world's plant and animal species live in rain forests or originally came from rain forests. Scientists continue to discover plants in the rain forests that have medicinal value (useful for treating medical problems). In fact, over 25 percent of the medicines we have come from rain forest plants. And there are still a lot of plants to find.

The Effects of Rain Forests on the Earth's Climate

B   But rain forests are important not only for the plants and animals that live in them and for the medicines that come from them. They also have major effects on the earth's atmosphere and climate. According to some scientists, global warming is causing dangerous changes to the earth's climate. Rain forests can help us fight global warming. Some scientists believe that rain forests cool the atmosphere by absorbing the sun's heat. *Absorb* means to soak up. Also, plants and trees use carbon dioxide. The cause of global warming is an increase of gases like carbon dioxide in our atmosphere. So rain forests can clean some of the excess (extra) carbon dioxide out of the air.

How We Are Destroying Rain Forests

C   Rain forests are so important to the earth, but we are cutting them down and burning them very quickly. Why? Some companies want to use the trees to make wood and paper. Others want to use the land to raise animals or grow crops (plants that farmers grow to use as food). This is dangerous for the climate in two ways. First, we are destroying something that helps cool down the earth's atmosphere. And second, by burning rain forests, we add a lot of carbon dioxide to the air. In fact, the burning of rain forests is responsible for about 30 percent of the carbon dioxide in our atmosphere. Some people believe that in 40 years, all the rain forests will be destroyed. What will happen to the earth's climate when all the rain forests are gone?

1. What is the main idea of this article?

(A) Rain forests are important because they are very old and most of our medicines come from their plants.

(B) We need to protect rain forests because they are important to the earth in many ways.

(C) We are destroying the rain forests very quickly.

(D) The rain forests are important, but they do not have a major effect on the earth's climate.

2. In some rain forests, _____

(A) the trees grow to 33 feet.

(B) there are no animals because there is so much rain.

(C) 33 feet of rain falls each year.

(D) 25 percent of the plants can be used for medicine.

3. Rain forests can be helpful to the earth because _____

(A) they heat the atmosphere.

(B) they put carbon dioxide into the atmosphere.

(C) they burn the carbon dioxide in the atmosphere.

(D) they soak up the carbon dioxide in the atmosphere.

4. Scientists and researchers probably _____

(A) are still looking for medicinal plants in rain forests.

(B) are not looking for medicinal plants in the rain forests anymore.

(C) don't believe there are any more important plants to find in the rain forests.

(D) all agree that global warming is harming the earth's atmosphere.

5. Burning rain forests _____

(A) helps farmers grow strong crops.

(B) adds carbon dioxide to the air.

(C) cools the atmosphere.

(D) cools the carbon dioxide in the air.

Section II Strategy Summarize Paragraph B from the reading "The Effects of Rain Forests on the Earth's Climate." Remember these suggestions as you write your summary **(15 points)**

❑   In English, think about the meaning of the information.

❑   In your own words, begin with the most general point about the paragraph topic. Tell the main idea in your own words.

❑   Then give only the important supporting details (definitions, examples, facts, and reasons) for that point.

❑   To shorten your summary, put similar ideas in the same sentence.

_____

_____

_____

_____

_____

Scoring Guidelines:

5 points maximum for a clear and correct topic sentence

5 points maximum for a clear and correct main idea

5 points maximum for correct supporting details

Section III New Words Fill in the blanks with words from the box below. **(4 points each)**

atmosphere	carbon dioxide	damage	diseases	effects
extreme	rain	scientists	affect	increase

Some _____ believe that global warming is changing our earth's climate. Some
            1

of the _____ of global warming are strong winds and hurricanes in some places
          2

and droughts in other places. This kind of _____ weather can cause major
                                              3

_____ to people's homes. Scientists say that the _____ in
          4   5

gases like _____ are the cause of global warming.
              6

Rain forests can help us fight global warming. They can _____ the climate in
                                                            7

good ways. For example, they cool the _____ and remove carbon dioxide from
                                          8

the air.

Rain forests are important to the earth in other ways, too. There are many medicinal plants in the

rain forest. Medicines made from these plants help people with serious _____
                                                                            9

and health problems. Rain forests usually get more than 33 feet of _____
                                                                      10

each year, so you might not want to live in one. But most of the animal species on earth live

in rain forests. For all of these reasons, it's important to protect the rain forests and stop

destroying them.

Section IV Vocabulary and Language Learning Skills Complete the sentences below with words from the reading "Rain Forests and the Earth's Climate." Some definitions are in the context following *be* or *mean*; some are in parentheses ( ). There are also words with the same or similar meanings. The letters in parentheses refer to the paragraphs of the reading. **(4 points each)**

1. These areas of land get a lot of rainfall and are covered by tall trees. They are

   _____. (A)

2. This word means "to find." It is _____. (A)

3. Some plants are useful for treating medical problems. They have _____. (A)

4. This word means "extra." It is _____. (B)

5. Another word for "soak up" is _____. (B)

TOTAL _____ /100 pts.

Name _____ Date _____ Score _____

Chapter 3 Test

Making Smart Fast-Food Choices

Section I Reading Comprehension Read the passage. Then answer the questions that follow.
(5 points each)

Fast Food Can Be Good Food

A Many people are too busy to prepare and eat three nutritious meals a day. So they turn to the convenience of fast-food restaurants. Many of the items at fast-food restaurants, snack bars, and food stands are fattening and not very nutritious. But fast food doesn't have to be unhealthy. You can eat at fast-food restaurants and still eat well.

Pay Attention to Calories and Fat Content

B By paying attention to the number of calories and fat that a food item has, you can make smarter choices. *Calories* are "units for measuring how much energy a food will produce." Consider two fast-food meals. A quarter-pound hamburger with cheese, jumbo-size fries, and a 16-ounce soda have a total of 1,535 calories and 76 grams of fat. A broiled (cooked under direct heat or over a flame) chicken sandwich, a side salad with low-fat dressing, and a glass of water at the same fast-food restaurant have only 422 calories and 7 grams of fat. But maybe you really want a hamburger and fries. Well, you can have a small hamburger, a small serving of fries, and a glass of water. At a total of 490 calories and 20 grams of fat, that's still a much smarter choice than the large burger, fries, and soda.

There's More That You Can Do

C There are a few additional things you can do to make sure you eat well in fast food restaurants. First of all, say "no" when the cashier asks you if you want to "supersize" your meal (order an extra large portion of each item). Second, ask for no mayonnaise or sauce, or ask for it on the side (in a separate dish). Third, substitute (use something instead of something else) healthy foods for fatty ones. For example, instead of ordering deep-fried tempura, order fresh vegetables. Instead of ordering a beef burrito with lots of cheese and sour cream, order a vegetable burrito with beans and rice. And don't eat the chips! Another thing you can do is order a side salad or a vegetable soup and eat it first. That way, you'll eat some vegetables, and you won't be able to eat as much of your burger and fries. Finally, eat slowly and stop eating when you're full. It sounds simple, but many people keep eating even after they become full.

1. What is the main idea of this article?
   (A) It's smart to eat foods with low calories and fat content.
   (B) You can eat well in fast-food restaurants.
   (C) Fast food is always bad for you.
   (D) Fast-food restaurants are the best place to find healthy foods.

2. A small hamburger and small fries has _____
   (A) more calories and fat than a chicken sandwich and a salad.
   (B) fewer calories and fat than a chicken sandwich and a salad.
   (C) the same amount of calories and fat as a chicken sandwich and a salad.
   (D) the same amount of calories and fat as a large portion of fries.

3. Some things you can do to eat well in fast-food restaurants are _____
   (A) ask for extra mayonnaise and sauce and say no to "supersizing".
   (B) order smaller portions and eat all the food you order.
   (C) order healthy foods instead of fatty ones and drink water.
   (D) order a vegetable burrito instead of chips and eat sour cream.

4. Mayonnaise and sauces probably _____
   (A) make you eat more because they make your food taste better.
   (B) don't have a lot of fat and calories.
   (C) have a lot of fat and calories.
   (D) make you eat less because they make you feel full sooner.

5. By eating a salad or soup before the rest of your meal, _____
   (A) you get full sooner.
   (B) you eat less of the rest of your meal.
   (C) you eat more slowly.
   (D) you eat the rest of your meal more quickly.

Section II Strategy Three of the items below are main ideas from the article "Making Smart Fast-Food Choices." Two of them are supporting details. Match each main idea with the related paragraph. Write the letter of the paragraph on the line next to the main idea. Write "SD" next to the items that are supporting details. **(5 points each)**

1. _____ For fewer calories and fat, you can substitute healthy foods for fatty ones.

2. _____ There are   other things you can do to make sure you eat good food in fast-food

   restaurants.

3. _____ You can eat well at fast-food restaurants.

4. _____ Paying attention to the calories and fat content in foods can help you make good food choices.

5. _____ Stop eating when you're full.

Section III New Words Fill in the blanks with words from the Word List below. **(3 points each)**

complex carbohydrates	customs	dairy	diabetes	diet
elements	frozen	habits	minerals	soy products

The word _____ has more than one basic meaning. It can mean "a person's

1

or a group's usual food choices and _____." Or it can mean "an eating plan

2

with only certain kinds or amounts of food." Individuals usually make their diet choices based

on old habits, cost, convenience, and beliefs about health, nutrition, and beauty. Some people

believe that natural food is the best, so they opt for fresh rather than _____

3

foods. Others have health problems and have to watch what they eat. For example, people with

_____ are usually on non-sugar diets.

4

The diets of cultures and regions aren't based on these things. Instead, these diets are based on

location, history, _____, and tradition. The Mexican diet includes foods from

5

pre-Columbian, Spanish, and French cultures. It contains a lot of _____, such

6

as corn, beans, and rice. Fish and _____, such as tofu, are common in the

7

Japanese diet. The Jewish diet is based on religious practices. Jewish people cannot eat meat and

_____ products like milk and cheese at the same meal. Muslims follow the laws

8

of halaal. They can eat only permitted foods.

Even with all these differences in individual and cultural diets, more and more meals all over the

world include the basic necessary food _____. And most dishes contain the

9

important vitamins and _____ that we need to stay healthy.

10

Section IV Vocabulary and Language Learning Skills Write the words from the list under the correct category in the chart below. **(2 points each)**

| carbohydrates | cholesterol | convenience | dairy | fats |
| fried | nutritious | protein | soy products | tradition |

Kinds of Food	Elements in Food	Reasons for Choosing Foods

TOTAL _____ /100 pts.

Name _____ Date _____ Score _____

Chapter 4 Test

Mapping Websites: How Do They Work?

Section I Reading Comprehension Read the passage. Then answer the questions that follow.
(5 points each)

A   These days, it's getting easier and easier to find your way around. Some people have GPS devices in their cars to make sure they don't get lost. GPS stands for Global Positioning System. These devices use satellites in space to "see" where you are and give you directions to where you want to go. And if you don't have a GPS device, you can simply go online to get step-by-step directions. Websites like MapQuest.com and mappoint.msn.com can produce a map and directions in just a few seconds. But how do they do it?

B   MapQuest® uses data (information) from a few different sources to produce directions and maps. Before MapQuest® went online, it sold regular paper maps in places like gas stations. The website uses the data from those paper maps, information from digital mapping companies, and government databases. At the moment, MapQuest® uses more than 30 computers to read all this data and provides users with millions of maps every day.

C   In order to find the best route (way or path) from one place to another, MapQuest® first has to look at all possible routes. Then MapQuest® looks at each part of each possible route. It considers the types of roads on the different routes. Are they dirt roads, paved roads, freeways, or city streets? It looks at how many turns there are in each route and what kinds of turns they are. Are they right turns or left turns? It also considers the speed limit on each road and how many intersections there are. An *intersection* is "a place where two or more roads cross each other."

D   MapQuest® can also tell you how long your trip will take you. It does this by doing some math. MapQuest® bases its estimated driving times on the length and speed limit of each part of the route and the amount of time it probably takes to get through each intersection. For example, it allows more time for a left turn at an intersection than it does for a right turn. Someday, maybe we will have cars that can just drive us wherever we want to go, but for now, mapping websites make it a little harder to get lost.

Source: http://www.howstuffworks.com/MapQuest.htm.

1. What is the main idea of this article?

    (A) Why mapping websites don't work well.

    (B) Why mapping websites are better than paper maps.

    (C) How the first mapping website started.

    (D) How mapping websites work.

2. According to the article, MapQuest® _____

    (A) started as an Internet company.

    (B) starting by selling paper maps.

    (C) started as maker of government databases.

    (D) uses millions of computers to read data.

3. When you search for directions, the first thing MapQuest® does is _____

    (A) estimate driving time.

    (B) consider how many turns you want to take.

    (C) look at all possible paths.

    (D) print out a map and directions.

4. When it's deciding on the best route, MapQuest® probably chooses _____

    (A) city streets instead of freeways.

    (B) the route with the most turns.

    (C) dirt roads instead of paved roads.

    (D) freeways instead of dirt roads.

5. To estimate your driving time, MapQuest® considers _____

    (A) the speed limit for half of the route.

    (B) the fastest and slowest speed limits on your route.

    (C) the speed limits and types of turns on your route.

    (D) the distance between turns on your route.

Section II Strategy In the article "Mapping Web Sites: How Do They Work," there is a capital letter next to each paragraph. Write the specific topic of each paragraph next to its letter. Write the topic of the entire article on the last line. **(5 points each)**

A. _____.

B. _____.

C. _____.

D. _____.

Whole reading: _____.

Section III New Words Match each vocabulary item on the left with an item on the right that has the same (or a similar) meaning. **(3 points each)**

1. _____ laws   **a.** many

2. _____ procedure   **b.** walkers

3. _____ pedestrians   **c.** cars

4. _____ travelers   **d.** rules

5. _____ (a) lot   **e.** rarely

6. _____ illegal   **f.** gesture

7. _____ motion   **g.** way

8. _____ seldom   **h.** places

9. _____ landmarks   **i.** wrong

10. _____ vehicles   **j.** tourists

Section IV Vocabulary and Language Learning Skills How do the items below belong together. Do they have the same (similar) meanings or are they members of the same category? Write S for similar meaning and C for category on the line, and name the possible category. **(2 points each)**

1. _____ South America / Asia / Europe   Possible category:_____

2. _____ teenagers / young people / youth   Possible category:_____

3. _____ cars / buses / trucks   Possible category:_____

4. _____ fine / money / charge   Possible category:_____

5. _____ odd / unusual / strange   Possible category:_____

6. _____ left / right / straight   Possible category:_____

7. _____ wine / milk / water   Possible category:_____

8. _____ robbery / murder / violence   Possible category:_____

9. _____ polite / friendly / nice   Possible category:_____

10. _____ restaurant / hotel / bus stop   Possible category:_____

TOTAL _____ **/100 pts.**

Chapter 5 Test

The Industrial Revolution and Its Impact on Our Lives Today

Section I Reading Comprehension Read the passage. Then answer the questions that follow. **(5 points each)**

Introduction

A The Industrial Revolution was a period of time when machines were invented and the first factories were opened. Machines created industry. In other words, machines made it possible to produce a large number of goods very quickly. This industrialization caused major changes in family life, the lives of individuals, and the culture of Western Europe and North America in the late 18th and early 19th centuries. It is also largely responsible for the way many people live today.

A Movement to the Cities

B First of all, industrialization moved people into the cities. Before the Industrial Revolution, many families lived in the country. They grew their own food and worked at home. Husbands and wives shared the work, and their children helped. But when factories started to open, people began to buy goods from big companies, and not from individual people. For example, machines made cloth much more quickly than weavers (people who make cloth) did. This made the cloth less expensive. So people began to buy factory-made cloth, and weavers lost their customers. Because of this, many families had to move to cities and get jobs.

A Shift in Family Life

C Industrialization also caused a major change in family life. In the city, one person in the family had to work outside of the home and one person had to stay home to take care of the children. The women were able to breastfeed the children, so they stayed home while the men worked in the factories. This was the start of the traditional family—a stay-at-home mother, a working father, and their children.

Availability of Newspapers and Books

D Another major result of the Industrial Revolution was the mass production of newspapers and books. Before industrialization, books and newspapers had to be printed by hand, so they were very expensive. Machines printed newspapers and books quickly and inexpensively, so more people were able to buy them. This change caused at least two important effects. First, it created a bigger need for literacy (the ability to read and write). Second, it increased public involvement in politics. Now anyone with a few cents could buy a newspaper and learn about the politics of their countries and cities. In most countries today, we expect to learn to read, and we expect to know what our governments are doing.

1. What is the main idea of this article?
- (A) Changes during the Industrial Revolution affect our lives today.
- (B) The Industrial Revolution caused many people to move from the country to the city.
- (C) The Industrial Revolution was a period when machines were invented and factories were opened.
- (D) Machines made life easier for everyone during the late 18th and early 19th centuries.

2. Industrialization was probably _____
- (A) good for individual book printers.
- (B) bad for individual book printers.
- (C) good for weavers.
- (D) bad for factory owners.

3. One effect of industrialization was that _____
- (A) many people began to grow their own food.
- (B) some people had to work at home.
- (C) a lot of people had to get factory jobs.
- (D) nobody was able to find a job.

4. Another effect of industrialization was that _____
- (A) more people read books and newspapers.
- (B) people didn't have time to read books and newspapers anymore.
- (C) books were invented.
- (D) people spent all their money on books and newspapers.

5. The word "industry" means _____
- (A) the invention of machines.
- (B) a major shift in culture and in lives of individuals.
- (C) the way people live.
- (D) the quick production of a large number of goods.

Section II Strategy In the article "The Industrial Revolution and Its Impact on Our Lives Today," there is a capital letter next to each paragraph. Write the specific topic of each paragraph next to its letter. Write the topic of the entire article on the last line. **(5 points each)**

A. _____.

B. _____.

C. _____.

D. _____.

Whole reading: _____.

Section III New Words Match each vocabulary item on the left with an item on the right that has the opposite meaning. **(3 points each)**

1. _____ divorces   **a.** awake

2. _____ decline   **b.** increase

3. _____ birthrate   **c.** working mother

4. _____ future   **d.** developing

5. _____ asleep   **e.** private

6. _____ master   **f.** marriages

7. _____ stay-at-home mother   **g.** servant

8. _____ communal   **h.** worsen

9. _____ industrialized   **i.** percent of deaths

10. _____ improve   **j.** past

Section IV Vocabulary and Language Learning Skills Below are some sentences with related words—nouns and adjectives—in parentheses. Circle the correct word form. Then write "noun" or "adjective" on the lines for each word you circled. **(4 points each)**

_____ 1. In the late 18th century, Western Europe became (industry/industrialized).

_____ 2. Some people felt that industrialization was an (improved/improvement), but some people thought it was a bad thing for society.

_____ 3. The Industrial Revolution was an important (history/historical) event.

_____ 4. The Industrial Revolution was responsible for a lot of major (developments/ developed) in society.

_____ 5. Cities became very (crowds/crowded) during the Industrial Revolution.

TOTAL _____ /100 pts.

Chapter 6 Test

Cross-Cultural Business Blunders

Section I Reading Comprehension Read the passage. Then answer the questions that follow.
(5 points each)

A Many visitors to different countries don't realize how important it is to understand a country's culture. Sometimes people learn this lesson by making a big cross-cultural blunder, or embarrassing mistake. In business situations, these blunders can cost a lot of money or end business relationships.

B When companies are trying to sell products, it's very important for them to understand what is important to their potential customers, and to understand a bit of their language. For example, one company wanted to sell toothpaste in Southeast Asia. In their advertisements, they claimed that their toothpaste whitens teeth. They didn't understand that many of the local people chewed betel nuts to make their teeth black, and that these people thought black teeth were attractive. In another case, a car company tried to sell a car called "Matador" in a Spanish-speaking country. The company thought that it was a strong name because it means "bullfighter." In Spanish, matador is indeed a noun meaning "bullfighter." But it is also an adjective meaning "killing." Imagine driving around in a car called "Killing"!

C Business meetings with people from another country can be very tricky when you don't understand the other country's culture. A European businessman had an important meeting with a company in Taiwan. He wanted to bring gifts for the people he was meeting with. He thought that something with his company's logo on it would be a nice gift. So he bought some very nice pocket knives and had his company's logo printed on them. He didn't know that giving a knife as a gift symbolizes cutting off a friendship! The Taiwanese businessmen were very offended (angry and upset). But luckily, the European businessman was able to repair the relationship with a lot of explanation and apology.

D It's very easy to make blunders like these people did. But it's also very easy not to. Before you visit a new country, research that country's customs and etiquette (social rules for polite behavior). You can find a lot of information online. Just go to a search engine and type in key words like "cross-cultural etiquette" or "cultural information Taiwan." By spending a few minutes doing research, you can save yourself from a lot of embarrassment and make sure you don't accidentally offend anyone.

http://www.cyborlink.com/besite

1. What is the main idea of this article?
- (A) People in Southeast Asia like to chew betel nuts.
- (B) It's important to understand other people's cultures before you do business with them.
- (C) It's dangerous to understand other people's cultures before you do business with them.
- (D) Proper business etiquette in most countries is difficult for foreigners to understand.

2. The toothpaste company probably _____
- (A) changed their advertisement in Southeast Asia.
- (B) tried to convince people in Southeast Asia that betel nuts are bad for your teeth.
- (C) kept using the same advertisement in Southeast Asia.
- (D) started to sell cars instead of toothpaste.

3. The car company that tried to sell a car to a Spanish-speaking country probably _____
- (A) sold a lot of Matador cars in that country.
- (B) changed the name of the car to "Killing."
- (C) didn't sell many Matador cars in that country.
- (D) were offended by their potential customers.

4. The European businessman probably _____
- (A) researches new cultures before he visits them now.
- (B) doesn't do business in Taiwan anymore.
- (C) always brings pocket knives as gifts to business meetings.
- (D) didn't care that he offended the Taiwanese businessmen.

5. What can you do to save yourself from making cross-cultural blunders?
- (A) You can't do anything.
- (B) You can disagree with people when they say you did something wrong.
- (C) You can teach people from other countries how you do things in *your* culture.
- (D) You can do research on the Internet.

Section II Strategy   The article "Cross-Cultural Business Blunders," contains three anecdotes. Below are five possible topics that are about the anecdotes. Two of the topics do not describe the anecdotes. Write the letter of each topic next to the description of the anecdote. Then write a sentence or two summarizing each anecdote. **(5 points each)**

a. email etiquette

b. language

c. gift-giving

d. advertising

e. explaining and apologizing

_____ **1.** toothpaste and betel nuts

Summary: _____

_____ **2.** car

Summary: _____

_____

_____ **3.** pocket knives

Summary: _____

_____

Scoring Guidelines: 1 point for choosing the letter of the correct topic.

4 points for each summary.

Section III New Words Match each vocabulary item on the left with its definition on the right.
(3 points each)

1. _____ architecture   **a.** wonderful, incredible

2. _____ civilization   **b.** visual, sound, and printed ways to send ideas

3. _____ media   **c.** to say that someone's ideas are wrong

4. _____ invented   **d.** in a believable way

5. _____ amazing   **e.** the form and plan of buildings

6. _____ attention   **f.** not polite

7. _____ rude   **g.** interest or focus

8. _____ convincingly   **h.** culture

9. _____ patiently   **i.** calmly, without becoming angry or anxious

10. _____ contradict   **j.** created something new that didn't exist before

Section IV Vocabulary and Language Learning Skills Below are some sentences with related words—nouns, verbs, and adjectives—in parentheses. Circle the correct word form. Then write "noun", "verb" or "adjective" on the lines for each word you circled. **(6 points each)**

Scoring Guidelines: 3 points for circling the correct word form.

3 points for writing the correct part of speech.

_____ **1.** The whole dinner was delicious, and the dessert was (excellence/excels/excellent)!

_____ **2.** Ancient Asian and Middle Eastern cultures were very (invention/invents/inventive). They created mathematics, writing, and the first calendar.

_____ **3.** I had many wonderful (experiences/experience/experienced) in my business meetings because I studied Japanese culture before my trip!

_____ **4.** When you (opposition/oppose/opposing) something someone says, it's important to disagree politely.

_____ **5.** There are so many (contradictions/contradict/contradictory) in your argument! What do you really think?

TOTAL _____ /100 pts.

Chapter 7 Test

The Internet as a Medical Resource: Helpful or Dangerous?

Section I Reading Comprehension Read the passage. Then answer the questions that follow. **(5 points each)**

A Because of the convenience of the Internet, people are taking more responsibility for their own health these days. This can be very beneficial. For instance, a doctor doesn't always have time to thoroughly explain an illness. In these cases, the Internet can be a valuable resource—a place to read all about the causes, symptoms, and remedies for an illness. A patient can also join an online group where he or she can chat with other people with the same illness. These people might be able to offer advice or help the patient get through a difficult time.

B Many remedies, or cures, that you can find online may or may not be helpful, but they may not be harmful either. For example, some websites claim that sniffing (smelling) a newspaper can cure nausea (the feeling of being sick to your stomach and wanting to vomit). Other websites suggest that a person with a cold should keep a piece of raw garlic in his or her mouth all day and bite down on it every few minutes to release the juice. People with smelly feet are told to soak their feet in tea for half an hour. These remedies might be unpleasant or odd, but they probably won't cause any harm. And who knows? They might actually be helpful.

C However, the Internet can be a dangerous tool if a patient isn't careful. Unfortunately, some of the "remedies" that are sold online are not only useless, they can also be harmful. For example, many labels claim that herbal remedies are "100 percent natural," so people think they are safe to take. But some of these herbs can cause serious problems when they are mixed with other drugs. For instance, an herbal remedy for helping your memory may also be a blood thinner. So if your doctor prescribed (put you on) a blood thinner and you start taking this herb without asking your doctor about it, a simple cut could be deadly; you might not be able to stop bleeding.

D The bottom line is this: be careful when using the Internet as a health resource. Use it to find information that you can discuss with your doctor. But don't spend a lot of money on "miracle cures." For example, don't believe outrageous claims that a pill can cure your illness in a week, or help you lose ten pounds in ten days. If something sounds too good to be true, it probably is.

1. What is the main idea of this article?

    Ⓐ You should always use the Internet as a resource before visiting a doctor.

    Ⓑ The Internet can be a helpful resource, but it can also be harmful.

    Ⓒ Miracle cures are always dangerous.

    Ⓓ It's important to be responsible for your own health because doctors don't have time.

2. One benefit of using the Internet as a medical resource is _____

    Ⓐ you can sell miracle cures to people in chat groups.

    Ⓑ you can talk with doctors about your illness or disease.

    Ⓒ doctors go there to thoroughly explain illnesses to patients.

    Ⓓ it has a lot of information about illnesses and diseases.

3. One possible remedy for nausea is _____

    Ⓐ smelling a newspaper.

    Ⓑ soaking your feet in garlic tea.

    Ⓒ drinking a lot of tea.

    Ⓓ biting down on raw garlic.

4. A person who is taking a prescribed drug should probably _____

    Ⓐ take only small amounts of herbal remedies.

    Ⓑ take herbal remedies to make the drug work faster.

    Ⓒ stop taking the drug if he or she finds an herbal remedy that works better.

    Ⓓ talk to the doctor before taking an herbal remedy.

5. The best way to use the Internet as a medical resource is to _____

    Ⓐ use it to look for free miracle cures that your doctor won't discuss with you.

    Ⓑ find cheap medications that your doctor prescribes to you.

    Ⓒ read about your illness and discuss what you find out with your doctor.

    Ⓓ learn how to safely mix prescription drugs with herbal remedies.

Section II Strategy Read and complete the mind map on the next page about "The Internet as a Medical Resource: Helpful or Dangerous?" Choose your answers from the phrases in the box after the diagram. **(3 points each)**

A Mind Map of "The Internet as a Medical Resource: Helpful or Dangerous?"

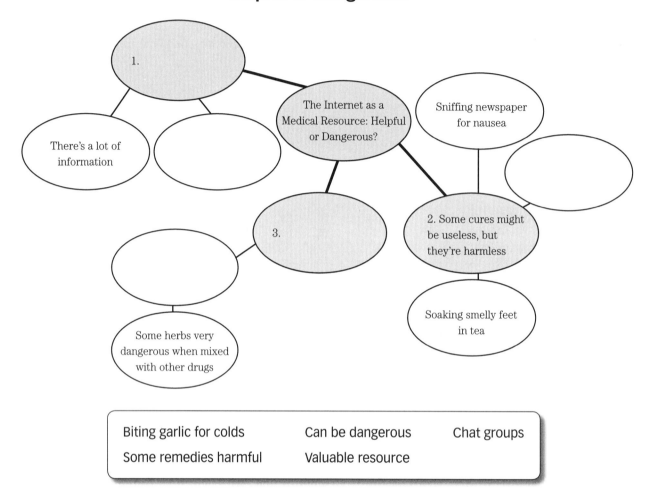

1.

There's a lot of information

The Internet as a Medical Resource: Helpful or Dangerous?

Sniffing newspaper for nausea

3.

2. Some cures might be useless, but they're harmless

Some herbs very dangerous when mixed with other drugs

Soaking smelly feet in tea

Biting garlic for colds	Can be dangerous	Chat groups
Some remedies harmful	Valuable resource	

Section III New Words Fill in the blanks with words from the Word List below. **(3 points each)**

claims	combination	cures	damage	decisions
diseases	dishonest	patients	proven	valid

It's important to be careful when using the Internet as a resource for medical information.

Not everyone tells the truth. In fact, some _____ people make a lot of
                                                    1

money by lying about their products. They make incredible _____ about
                                                              2

their miracle _____. They say that their remedies can help people with
              3

all kinds of different illnesses and _____. But most of the things they say
                                     4

aren't _____ to be true. And sometimes, the _____ of their
       5   6

herbal remedies with prescription drugs can do a lot of _____. They can

cause serious problems for _____. So be sure to make important medical
                                    8

_____ with your doctor. Your doctor will help you decide which claims are
         9

_____ and which are not accepted by the medical field.
       10

Section IV Vocabulary and Language Learning Skills On the line before each item below, indicate the part of speech: write *n* for noun, *adj* for adjective, or *adv* for adverb. Underline the ending (suffix) that indicates the part of speech. **(3 points each)**

1. _____ difference

2. _____ backward

3. _____ decision

4. _____ preventive

5. _____ agreeably

6. _____ sensible

7. _____ availability

8. _____ changeable

9. _____ ignorance

10. _____ religious

TOTAL _____**/100 pts.**

Chapter 8 Test

Television: The Latest Addiction

Section I Reading Comprehension Read the passage. Then answer the questions that follow. **(5 points each)**

A   Everyone has heard of addictions to drugs, cigarettes, alcohol, and even gambling. But can people become addicted to television? If so, how can an addiction to television damage a person's life?

B   It's very easy to understand how an addiction to cigarettes, drugs, or alcohol can be very damaging to a person's life. Cigarettes can cause illnesses like cancer and emphysema, a lung disease that makes it difficult to breathe. In addition to being bad for your health, alcohol and drugs can impair your ability to think clearly and behave responsibly. These substances can cause your life to slowly fall apart. In the worst cases, alcohol and drug addicts can lose their friends, families, jobs, and homes.

C   But how can watching too much television be harmful to your life and health? One way is that it can start a cycle of bad feelings. According to one study, people who watch the most TV already suffer from anxiety or loneliness. Watching TV makes them feel relaxed and helps them forget about their feelings for a while. But the study found that while people did relax while watching television, the feelings of relaxation disappeared after they stopped watching, and the people felt worse than they did when they started watching TV. Therefore, they wanted to watch more television so they could continue to forget their bad feelings. All this TV watching kept them from doing things that could actually make them feel better, like exercising, participating in hobbies, reading, or spending time with friends and family.

D   Another way TV watching can be harmful is, like the addictions mentioned above, TV can cause you to neglect your life. The more you watch, the more you want to watch, and after a while, TV replaces real experiences. TV addicts stop talking to their families, don't exercise, don't see their friends, and don't learn new things. Basically, TV addicts stop experiencing life.

E   The harmful effects of TV addiction may not be as obvious as those of cigarette, drug, or alcohol addiction, but TV addiction can take a person's life away. If you think that excessive TV watching is not harmful, keep track of how much TV you watch every day, and think about all the other things you could be doing during those wasted hours.

1. What is the main idea of this article?

    Ⓐ TV addictions are more dangerous than cigarette, alcohol, and drug addictions.

    Ⓑ TV addiction is not harmful to your life at all.

    Ⓒ TV addiction can be harmful to your life.

    Ⓓ People watch a lot of TV, but there is no such thing as a TV addiction.

2. According to the article, one way cigarette smoking can be harmful to your life is that _____

    Ⓐ it can make you neglect your friends and family.

    Ⓑ it can cause you to lose more and more money until you become obsessed.

    Ⓒ it smells bad, so people won't want to spend time with you.

    Ⓓ it can cause serious health problems.

3. According to the article, one way drug and alcohol addiction can be harmful is that _____

    Ⓐ you can get emphysema, a disease of the lungs.

    Ⓑ addicts spend all their time trying to put their lives back together.

    Ⓒ it keeps addicts from doing things that make them feel better, like exercising.

    Ⓓ drugs and alcohol keep addicts from thinking clearly and being responsible.

4. According to a study, the people who watch the most TV _____

    Ⓐ like to watch shows that teach them new things.

    Ⓑ already feel bad about themselves and their lives.

    Ⓒ also spend the most time exercising.

    Ⓓ don't have jobs.

5. Television addicts probably _____

    Ⓐ are not healthy and physically fit.

    Ⓑ only watch shows that they really enjoy.

    Ⓒ feel better about themselves after relaxing in front of the TV.

    Ⓓ spend a lot of time with their friends.

Section II Strategy Complete the outline below for the article "Television: The Latest Addiction." Use the phrases in the box. **(3 points each)**

    ❏ Bad for your health, thinking, and behavior

    ❏ Effects of TV addiction may not be obvious

    ❏ Emphysema

    ❏ Starts a cycle of bad feelings

    ❏ Watching TV makes addicts feel worse

I. Introduction

II. Cigarette, drug, and alcohol addictions are harmful

  A. Cigarettes cause illnesses

    1. Cancer

    2. _____

B. Alcohol and drugs are bad for you

　1. _____

　2. Addicts lose friends, family, jobs, and homes

III. TV addiction is bad for you

　A. _____

　　1. TV addicts already feel anxious and depressed

　　2. _____

　　3. TV keeps them from doing things to feel better

　B. Causes addicts to neglect their lives

　　1. Addicts stop exercising, learning, spending time with friends and family

IV. Conclusion

　A. _____

　B. It takes addicts' lives away

Section III New Words Fill in the blanks with words from the box below. **(4 points each)**

addicted	addiction	adults	dissatisfied	emotional
exciting	reality	relationships	replace	viewers

Too much TV can be dangerous for both _____ and children. In fact,

many people are actually _____ to television the same way some people
　　　　　　　　　　　　　　　　2

are addicted to drugs or alcohol. Why do people watch so much TV? Some people may be

_____ with what they consider their boring lives. They may find what's
　　3

happening on the screen more _____ than what's happening in their own lives.
　　　　　　　　　　　　　　　　　　4

According to one study, _____ who watch the most television already have
　　　　　　　　　　　　　5

_____ problems such as anxiety and loneliness, and they watch TV to forget
　　6

their problems. Unfortunately however, their _____ causes them to forget
　　　　　　　　　　　　　　　　　　　　　7

about _____ with friends and family too. The more TV they watch, the less they
　　8

think about _____. The less they think about their real lives, the more they

₉

_____ their real lives with the lives of the people on the TV screen. TV may be

₁₀

fun and harmless for most of us, but for some people, TV addiction is a sad reality.

Section IV Vocabulary and Language Learning Skills On the line before each item below, indicate the part of speech: write *n* for noun, *v* for verb, and *adj* for adjective. Underline the ending (suffix) that indicates the part of speech. **(2 points each)**

1. _____ addicted

2. _____ adulthood

3. _____ specialist

4. _____ sadden

5. _____ natural

6. _____ nuclear

7. _____ computerized

8. _____ classify

9. _____ personalize

10. _____ careful

TOTAL _____ **/100 pts.**

Chapter 9 Test

Making Friends in a New City

Section I Reading Comprehension Read the passage. Then answer the questions that follow. **(4 points each)**

I graduated from college recently and moved to San Francisco by myself. While I was in college, it was really easy to meet new people. I met them in class, through friends, at parties, and at the library all the time. But "out in the real world," I was finding it really hard. I live in a big city, and it seems like everyone around me is busy or already has all the friends they want. I was feeling so discouraged and I didn't know what to do, so I called my sister for some advice.

My sister is four years older than I am, so she's been through all this already. She's been helping me with my problems all my life. When I explained my problem, she understood completely. She said, "Why don't you try meeting people online?"

"Online? Are you kidding?" I asked. "A friend of mine chatted with a guy online, and when she finally met him face to face, he was nothing like he said he was."

My sister laughed. "You don't have to look for dates online," she said. "But you can find other people like you—people who have just moved to town and want to make some new friends. When I first moved to New York after college, I found a book club and a softball team online. I met a lot of people that way."

"But you don't even like softball!" I said.

"I know," she replied. "But that didn't matter. I still had a lot of fun. You played volleyball in college. Why don't you look for a volleyball team to join? Or an art class? You haven't painted since college."

"Yeah! Oh, and I saw a website about volunteering the other day." I said. "I could volunteer for an organization here in San Francisco. I bet I could meet a lot of really nice people that way."

"That's a great idea!" my sister answered enthusiastically. "Hey, you might even meet the perfect guy."

"OK, now you're starting to sound like Mom," I said. "Thanks a lot for the advice. I'm going to go online right now and start searching for volleyball teams, art classes, and volunteer organizations. I'll let you know what happens. Will you be home tonight?"

"No, but I'll be here all day tomorrow, so give me a call," my sister replied. "Good luck!"

1. What was the writer's problem?
- Ⓐ She couldn't meet people at her new college.
- Ⓑ She couldn't meet people in her new city.
- Ⓒ She didn't want to meet people online.
- Ⓓ She didn't like to play softball anymore.

2. When she was in college, the writer met people _____
- Ⓐ at volleyball games.
- Ⓑ at parties and at the library.
- Ⓒ online and in classes.
- Ⓓ through friends and through her book club.

3. The writer's sister _____
- Ⓐ had the same problems when she finished college.
- Ⓑ didn't go to college, but understands the writer's problem.
- Ⓒ lives in the same city as the writer.
- Ⓓ doesn't have any advice for the writer.

4. The writer probably _____
- Ⓐ doesn't like to bother her sister with problems.
- Ⓑ has a boyfriend.
- Ⓒ doesn't have a computer.
- Ⓓ calls her sister for advice often.

5. The writer is probably going to _____
- Ⓐ join a softball team.
- Ⓑ call her sister later tonight.
- Ⓒ call her sister tomorrow.
- Ⓓ join a book club like her sister did.

Section II Strategy

A. In each of the following passages, circle the words that the underlined word or phrase refers to. **(4 points each)**

1. While I was in college, it was really easy to meet new people. I met <u>them</u> in class, through friends, at parties, and at the library all the time.

2. "When I first moved to New York after college, I found a book club and a softball team online. I met a lot of people <u>that way</u>."

3. "But you don't even like softball!" I said.

"I know," she replied. "But <u>that</u> didn't matter."

4. "I could volunteer for an organization here in San Francisco. I bet I could meet a lot of great people <u>that way</u>."

5. "Will you be home tonight?"

"No, but I'll be home all day tomorrow, so call me <u>then</u>," my sister replied.

B. Read the sentences below. Write a check mark (✓) on the line in front of the ideas that the author stated or implied. Write an X on the line in front of the ideas that the writer did not state or imply.

_____ **6.** The writer felt discouraged because she couldn't make any new friends.

_____ **7.** Her sister gives her discouraging advice all the time.

_____ **8.** At first, the writer thinks that meeting people online is a great idea.

_____ **9.** By the end of the conversation, the writer likes the idea of going online to meet people.

_____ **10.** The writer liked to paint while she was in college.

Section III New Words Fill in the blanks with words from the word list below. **(2 points each)**

arrange	discouraged	fortunately	guy	match
optimistic	perfect	replied	spouses	worried

Sometimes I get so _____ about my sister. She just moved to San Francisco

                   1

and she's having trouble meeting new people. She's usually a very _____

                   2

person—she's always positive even in difficult situations. But I know she's been feeling

_____ lately because she hasn't made any new friends.

    3

I told her to look for volleyball teams and art classes online. Also, I have some friends in

San Francisco and I asked them to _____ some meetings between my

               4

sister and some of their friends, especially their male friends! She hasn't had a date in a

long time, and I want to help her meet a nice _____. Some of my friends'

            5

_____have some great male friends. Maybe one of them knows the

    6

_____ _____ for my sister!

    7   8

_____, my sister is really outgoing and friendly, so I know she'll make some

    9

new friends very soon. In fact, the volleyball team she emailed yesterday _____

                                                         10

to her right away. She's going to start playing this weekend!

Section IV Vocabulary and Language Learning Skills Which of the words below contain a prefix with a negative meaning? Underline those prefixes and write *N* on the line before the word. Write X on the lines before the words without negative meanings. **(2 points each)**

1. _____ disrespect

2. _____ discourage

3. _____ illegal

4. _____ illustrate

5. _____ instant

6. _____ informal

7. _____ under

8. _____ unusual

9. _____ impolite

10. _____ important

TOTAL _____/100 pts.

Name _____ Date _____ Score _____

Chapter 10 Test

Fairness at the Olympic Games

Section I Reading Comprehension Read the passage. Then answer the questions that follow.
(5 points each)

Dear Editor,

Competition in Olympic sports is supposed to be fair. However, in judged sports, fairness is impossible. Therefore, judged sports should be banned from the Olympic games. A judged sport is any sport that requires judges to determine a winner. For example, gymnastics, figure skating, half pipe (snowboarding), and diving are all judged sports.

Why do I believe that judged sports should be eliminated from the Olympics? First of all, judges don't see everything. For example, a mistake in figure skating can happen in a fraction of a second. If a judge blinks or looks away for a moment, he or she might miss the mistake and give the skater a higher score than the skater deserves.

Second, two judges can disagree about which athlete gave the best performance. In sports in which the difference between gold and silver is usually a few hundredths of a point, this kind of subjectivity is unacceptable. Can anyone really say with certainty that a gymnast who receives a score of 9.825 is a better gymnast than one who scores 9.823?

Only objective sports should be allowed in the Olympics. If someone runs, skates, or skis faster than anyone else, that person is the unquestionable winner. That's how all Olympic sports should be.

Sincerely,

Mitch Jones

Dear Editor,

A lot of people claim that judged sports are subjective and should not be allowed in the Olympics. They feel that only sports that are measured objectively for things like speed, such as swimming, track, and skiing, should be allowed because judges can't be objective and fair. I disagree with these people. Why? I believe that no sport is 100% fair and objective.

First, some athletes may win because their equipment is better than their opponents' equipment. For example, in the 2000 summer Olympics, some swimmers wore controversial high-tech suits. The maker of the suit claimed that the fabric could make a swimmer 3% faster. No one could prove that this was true, but they couldn't prove that it wasn't true either.

Also, sports like downhill skiing and track are measured objectively, but the tracks aren't always fair to all competitors. For example, weather can change over the course of a competition. A competitor who skis in clear weather will ski much faster than one who skis in snowy weather.

If we eliminate unfairly judged sports from the Olympics, we have to eliminate them all. Let's stop arguing about this topic and just celebrate the talented athletes.

Regards,

Mei Yap

1. What does the writer of the first letter believe?

- (A) Objective sports should be eliminated from the Olympics.
- (B) Judged sports should be eliminated from the Olympics.
- (C) All sports are subjective.
- (D) All sports are objective.

2. What does the writer of the second letter believe?

- (A) Objective sports should be eliminated from the Olympics.
- (B) Judged sports should be eliminated from the Olympics.
- (C) All sports are subjective.
- (D) All sports are objective.

3. One reason that judged sports should *not* be allowed in the Olympics is that _____

- (A) judges are not qualified.
- (B) judges don't know what kinds of mistakes to look for.
- (C) no one knows how to determine the winners.
- (D) judges can have different opinions.

4. One argument against banning judged sports from the Olympics is that _____

- (A) a lot of people don't want to keep them in the Olympics.
- (B) there is no completely objective sport.
- (C) people should stop arguing about it.
- (D) objective sports are boring to watch.

5. Mei Yap probably _____

- (A) likes to watch the Olympic games.
- (B) doesn't like to watch the Olympic games.
- (C) doesn't know much about sports.
- (D) doesn't like swimming, track, and skiing.

Section II Strategy Identify each of the items below as an objective fact (*F*) or a subjective opinion (*O*). You may look back at the reading selection if necessary. **(5 points each)**

1. _____ Competition in Olympic sports is supposed to be fair. However, in judged sports, fairness is impossible.

2. _____ A judged sport is any sport that requires judges to determine a winner. For example, gymnastics, figure skating, half pipe (snowboarding), and diving are all judged sports.

3. _____ Second, two judges can disagree about which athlete gave the best performance. In sports in which the difference between gold and silver is usually a few hundredths of a point, this kind of subjectivity is unacceptable.

4. _____ For example, in the 2000 summer Olympics, some swimmers wore controversial high-tech suits.

The maker of the suit claimed that the fabric could make a swimmer 3% faster.

5. _____ If we eliminate subjective sports from the Olympics, we have to eliminate them all.

Section III New Words Fill in the blanks with words from the word list below. **(3 points each)**

| achievements | banned | compete | competition | conflict |
| fans | international | intolerable | opposition | solve |

The subject of judged sports in the Olympics is a source of _____ for some

sports _____. These people have strong opinions on the topic and just can't

agree with each other.

Some people think that judged sports should be _____ from the Olympic

games. They feel that such sports do not belong in an _____ event like the

Olympics. They believe that judged sports are too subjective and that it's impossible to determine

a clear winner in any judged sport _____. These people argue that subjectivity

is _____ when the difference between first and second place is usually just a

few hundredths of a point.

The _____ argues that no sport is completely fair. For example, they say that

one competitor's equipment might be better than another's. That could make the competition

unfair. They also note that sometimes, a few athletes have to _____ in bad

weather while others have good weather, which can make a big difference. According to these

people, banning judged sports is not going to _____ any unfairness problems.

They recommend that we stop arguing and just celebrate the _____ of the

amazing athletes who compete in the Olympic games.

Section IV Vocabulary and Language Learning Skills Look at the underlined prefix and other word parts, and match the following vocabulary items in Column A with their possible explanations in Column B. **(2 points each)**

1. _____ <u>con</u>tribute (verb)

a. a specific kind of conversation between two or more people

2. _____ <u>ex</u>it (verb)

b. a raise in position, such as a higher-ranking job title

3. _____ <u>co</u>-worker (noun)

c. to create again

4. _____ <u>inter</u>view (noun)

d. to fix something so it works again or is like new again

5. _____ <u>inter</u>mission (noun)

e. to leave or go out of a place

6. _____ <u>pre</u>pare (verb)

f. someone who works with someone else

7. _____ <u>pro</u>motion (noun)

g. to advance or move forward

8. _____ <u>pro</u>gress (verb)

h. a period of time between two parts of a show

9. _____ <u>re</u>-create (verb)

i. to give to something other people are also giving to

10. _____ <u>re</u>pair (verb)

j. to get something ready before you need it

TOTAL ____ /100 pts.

Chapter 1 Test Answer Key

Section I

1. B 2. D 3. A 4. B 5. D

Section II

1. C 2. A 3. B 4. D 5. SD

Section III

1. d 2. g 3. a 4. j 5. i 6. b 7. c 8. e 9. f 10. h

Section IV

1. job 2. method 3. exam 4. scholarship
5. homework

Chapter 2 Test Answer Key

Section I

1. B 2. C 3. D 4. A 5. B

Section II

Answers will vary. Possible summary: Rain forests
are important because they can help fight global
warming in two different ways. First, some scientists
say that rain forests absorb the heat of the sun. In
this way, they cool the earth's climate, which affects
global warming in a good way. Second, excess carbon
dioxide causes global warming. The plants and trees in
rain forests can clean extra carbon dioxide out of the
air.

Section III

1. scientists 2. effects 3. extreme; 4. damage
5. increase 6. carbon dioxide 7. affect 8. atmosphere
9. diseases 10. rain

Section IV

1. rain forests 2. discover 3. medicinal value
4. excess 5. absorb

Chapter 3 Test Answer Key

Section 1

1. B 2. A 3. C 4. C 5. B

Section II

1. SD 2. C 3. A 4. B 5. SD

Section III

1. diet 2. habits 3. frozen 4. diabetes 5. customs
6. complex carbohydrates 7. soy products 8. dairy
9. elements 10. minerals

Section IV

Kinds of Food: dairy, fried, soy products, nutritious

Elements in Food: cholesterol, fats, protein,
carbohydrates

Reasons for Choosing Foods: tradition, convenience

Chapter 4 Test Answer Key

Section I

1. D 2. B 3. C 4. D 5. C

Section II

Answers will vary. Possible answers: A. Introduction
to the reading. B. MapQuest® uses data from different
sources. C. MapQuest® looks at all possible routes to
find the best one. D. MapQuest® uses math to tell you
how long your trip will take. Whole reading: How do
websites like MapQuest.com and mappoint.msn.com
work?

Section III

1. d 2. g 3. b 4. j 5. a 6. i 7. f 8. e 9. h 10. c

Section IV

1. C (continents) 2. S 3. C (vehicles) 4. S 5. S
6. C (directions) 7. C (beverages/drinks) 8. C (offenses,
crimes) 9. S 10. C (landmarks/places)

Chapter 5 Test Answer Key

Section I

1. A 2. B 3. C 4. A 5. D

Section II

Answers will vary. Possible answers: A. The Industrial
Revolution caused many changes in life and culture
during the 18th and 19th centuries and is responsible
for the way we live today. B. Industrialization caused
people to move from the country to the city to get
factory jobs. C. Industrialization is responsible for the
start of the traditional family. D. During the Industrial

Revolution, books and newspapers were cheaper, so more people were able to read them. This helped increase the need for literacy and involvement in politics. Whole reading: Many of the changes that occurred because of the Industrial Revolution affect our lives today.

Section III

1. f 2. b 3. i 4. j 5. a 6. g 7. c 8. e 9. d 10. h

Section IV

1. industrialized, adjective 2. improvement, noun
3. historical, adjective 4. developments, noun
5. crowded, adjective

Chapter 6 Test Answer Key

Section I

1. B 2. A 3. C 4. A 5. D

Section II

Answers will vary. Possible answers: 1. d, A company didn't understand that some people in Southeast Asia chew betel nuts, which make their teeth black, and they think black teeth are attractive. In a toothpaste advertisement, the company said that their toothpaste whitens teeth. 2. b, A car company tried to sell a car in a Spanish-speaking country. They didn't know that their car's name, "Matador," can mean "killing" in Spanish. 3. c, A European businessman gave knives to Taiwanese businessmen as a gift. He didn't know that knives symbolize cutting off friendships.

Section III

1. e 2. h 3. b 4. j 5. a 6. g 7. f 8. d 9. i 10. c

Section IV

1. excellent, adjective 2. inventive, adjective
3. experiences, noun 4. oppose, verb
5. contradictions, noun

Chapter 7 Test Answer Key

Section I

1. B 2. D 3. A 4. D 5. C

Section II

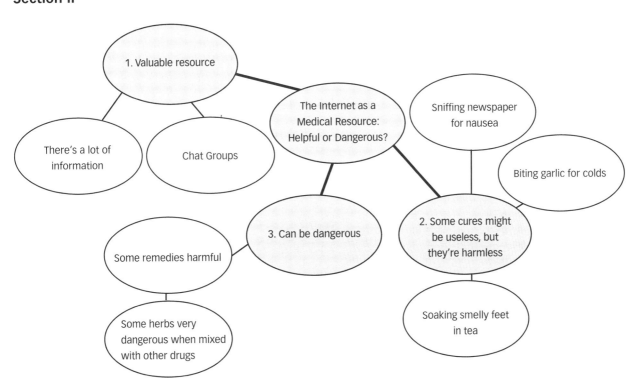

1. Valuable resource

There's a lot of information

Chat Groups

The Internet as a Medical Resource: Helpful or Dangerous?

Sniffing newspaper for nausea

Biting garlic for colds

3. Can be dangerous

Some remedies harmful

Some herbs very dangerous when mixed with other drugs

2. Some cures might be useless, but they're harmless

Soaking smelly feet in tea

Section III

1. dishonest 2. claims 3. cures 4. diseases 5. proven
6. combination 7. damage 8. patients 9. decisions
10. valid

Section IV

1. n, differ<u>ence</u> 2. adv, back<u>ward</u> 3. n, deci<u>sion</u>
4. adj, prevent<u>ive</u> 5. adv, agreeab<u>ly</u> 6. adj, sens<u>ible</u>
7. n, availabil<u>ity</u> 8. adj, change<u>able</u> 9. n, igno<u>rance</u>
10. adj, relig<u>ious</u>

Chapter 8 Test Answer Key

Section I

1. C 2. D 3. D 4. B 5. A

Section II

I. Introduction
II. Cigarette, drug, and alcohol addictions are harmful
    A. Cigarettes cause illnesses
        1. Cancer
        2. *Emphysema*
    B. Alcohol and drugs are bad for you
        1. *Bad for your health, thinking, and behavior*
        2. Addicts lose friends, family, jobs, and homes
III. TV addiction is bad for you
    A. *Starts a cycle of bad feelings*
        1. TV addicts already feel anxious and depressed
        2. *Watching TV makes addicts feel worse*
        3. TV keeps them from doing things to feel better
    B. Causes addicts to neglect their lives
        1. Addicts stop exercising, learning, spending time with friends and family
IV. Conclusion
    A. *Effects of TV addiction may not be obvious*
    B. It takes addicts' lives away

Section III

1. adults 2. addicted 3. dissatisfied 4. exciting
5. viewers 6. emotional 7. addiction 8. relationships
9. reality 10. replace

Section IV

1. adj, addict<u>ed</u> 2. n, adult<u>hood</u> 3. n, special<u>ist</u>
4. v, sadd<u>en</u> 5. adj, natur<u>al</u> 6. adj, nucle<u>ar</u> 7. adj,
computeriz<u>ed</u> 8. v, class<u>ify</u> 9. v, personal<u>ize</u> 10. adj,
care<u>ful</u>

Chapter 9 Test Answer Key

Section I

1. B 2. B 3. A 4. D 5. C

Section II

1. new people 2. I found a book club and a softball team online 3. you don't even like softball
4. volunteer for an organization 5. tomorrow
6. ✓ 7. X 8. X 9. ✓ 10. ✓

Section III

1. worried 2. optimistic 3. discouraged 4. arrange
5. guy 6. spouses 7. perfect 8. match 9. Fortunately
10. replied

Section IV

1. N dis 2. N dis 3. N il 4. X 5. X 6. N in 7. X 8. N un
9. N im 10. X

Chapter 10 Test Answer Key

Section I

1. B 2. C 3. D 4. B 5. A

Section II

1. O 2. F 3. O 4. F 5. O

Section III

1. conflict 2. fans 3. banned 4. international
5. competition 6. intolerable 7. opposition
8. compete 9. solve 10. achievements

Section IV

1. i 2. e 3. f 4. a 5. h 6. j 7. b 8. g 9. c 10. d

Reading Strand Placement Test
Vocabulary Section

Vocabulary I Choose the best word to complete each sentence. **(2 points each)**

Example: Brazil and Argentina are the largest _____ in South America.
- (A) categories
- (B) cities
- (C) countries
- (D) neighborhoods

1. No one lives with Rosa in her apartment. She lives _____.
   - (A) alone
   - (B) lonely
   - (C) only
   - (D) together

2. Tom's family has 3 children, Amy's family has 3 children, Reina's family has 2 children, and Ben's family has 2 children. The _____ number of children in these families is 2.5.
   - (A) small
   - (B) average
   - (C) equal
   - (D) total

3. When teachers speak too softly and rapidly, it is _____ for their students to understand them.
   - (A) easy
   - (B) little
   - (C) different
   - (D) difficult

4. In many cultures, women do most of the _____. For example, they clean the floors and wash the clothes for their families.
   - (A) farming
   - (B) homework
   - (C) housework
   - (D) cooking

5. Mr. Lee's restaurant is successful because he always waits on his _____ politely and serves them wonderful meals.
   - (A) customs
   - (B) customers
   - (C) consumers
   - (D) users

6. In a basketball game, two teams _____ against each other to score points by throwing a ball into a basket.
- Ⓐ compete
- Ⓑ cooperate
- Ⓒ complete
- Ⓓ exercise

7. In this country doctors usually have high _____ , or position in the society.
- Ⓐ profession
- Ⓑ situation
- Ⓒ state
- Ⓓ status

8. Many companies in the computer industry were started by very young people. For example, Bill Gates was only twenty years old when he and Paul Allen _____ the Microsoft Corporation in 1975.
- Ⓐ based
- Ⓑ discovered
- Ⓒ located
- Ⓓ founded

9. _____ up to 20% is customary in U.S. restaurants. Some places even add 15% to the bill for all parties of six or more.
- Ⓐ Waiting
- Ⓑ Tipping
- Ⓒ Buying
- Ⓓ Eating

10. I wouldn't go to the new mall just yet. If you can _____ another week or two, until the Grand Opening is over, the crowds will be much more manageable.
- Ⓐ hold out
- Ⓑ hold up
- Ⓒ wait on
- Ⓓ hold onto

Vocabulary II Read each item and then answer the vocabulary question below it. **(2 points each)**

Example: The city government recently announced plans to build a new road through Mountain Dale, a beautiful neighborhood on the south side of the city. The residents of Mountain Dale are angry about the road. Yesterday a group of them went to a meeting at City Hall to express their *views* on the city's plans.

Which of the following is closest in meaning to *views* as it is used above?
- Ⓐ pictures
- Ⓑ opinions
- Ⓒ sights
- Ⓓ beautiful scenery

1. The brain is divided into many parts. Each part serves specific and important functions. The cerebrum is the largest and most complex *area* of the brain. It controls thought, learning, and many other activities.
   Which of the following is closest in meaning to *area* as it is used above?
   - (A) the size of a surface, calculated by multiplying the length by the width
   - (B) a particular subject or group of related subjects
   - (C) a particular part or section
   - (D) a part of an activity or a thought

2. By studying the pyramids of Egypt, researchers have learned a great deal about ancient Egyptian *culture*. They have discovered, for example, that different social classes existed even in the earliest cities.
   Which of the following is closest in meaning to *culture* as it is used above?
   - (A) activities that are related to art, music, and literature
   - (B) a society that existed at a particular time in history
   - (C) a scientific experiment of people from a particular country
   - (D) education of people in a certain social group

3. Timothy is going to ride his bike around the world. In order to see all the countries and sights he wants to, before he begins his adventure, he will *map* his route.
   Which of the following is the closest in meaning to *map* as used above?
   - (A) to pack bags for a trip
   - (B) to plan the path of a trip
   - (C) to prepare a bicycle for a trip
   - (D) to talk about something

4. With today's computer networks, the *transmission* of data from one place in the world to another can happen instantly.
   Which of the following is closest in meaning to *transmission* as it is used above?
   - (A) the process of working together on the same computer network
   - (B) a job that involves traveling from one place to another
   - (C) the set of parts of a vehicle that take power from the engine to the wheels
   - (D) the process of sending information using electronic equipment

5. Roger has some annoying tendencies. For one thing, he's *inclined* to talk about himself and his achievements.
   Which of the following is closest in meaning to *inclined* as it is used above?
   - (A) bending forward to say something
   - (B) likely to do something or behave in a particular way
   - (C) holding a particular opinion
   - (D) talking a lot about the same thing

6. At medical centers throughout the United States, researchers are *conducting* investigations into the causes of heart disease.
   Which of the following is closest in meaning to *conducting* as it is used above?
   - (A) carrying out an activity or process in order to get information or prove facts
   - (B) directing the playing of an orchestra, band, etc.
   - (C) carrying something like electricity or heat to cure heart disease
   - (D) guiding or leading someone somewhere

7. In recent years, it seems that headlines and articles about war and violence have *occupied* the front pages of newspapers everywhere.

   Which of the following is closest in meaning to *occupied* as it is used above?

   (A) taken up time

   (B) lived in a place

   (C) controlled a place by military force

   (D) filled a particular amount of space

8. Studies in public schools have shown that *exposure* to art and music has many benefits for children. It improves their literacy, critical thinking, and math skills.

   Which of the following is closest in meaning to *exposure* as it is used above?

   (A) a situation in which someone is not protected from risk or danger

   (B) attention that someone gets from newspapers, television, etc.

   (C) the chance to experience something

   (D) the act of showing something that is usually hidden

9. Ronald and James are roommates in a university dormitory. They have frequent arguments because Ronald prefers to go to sleep early and James always stays up late. Also, Ronald likes quiet while he studies, but James insists that loud music helps him concentrate. How can James and Ronald *resolve* these conflicts?

   Which of the following is closest in meaning to *resolve* as it is used above?

   (A) make a definite decision to do something

   (B) solve again using new techniques

   (C) gradually change into something else

   (D) find a satisfactory way of dealing with a problem or difficulty

10. It is important that students learn to read and write before they go to college. In particular, they need to practice reading on their own and learn how to write a *succinct* and logical argument.

    Which of the following is the closest in meaning to *succinct* as used above?

    (A) taking a long time to explain

    (B) correct

    (C) original

    (D) clearly and concisely expressed

Reading Section

Directions: Read each passage and answer the questions below it. **(2 points each)**

Reading Passage I

A   How do you react to the taste of different foods, like coffee or lemon? Do they have a flavor that you like? Or do they taste very strong to you? Why do people react differently to different flavors?

B   We all know that different people have different food preferences. Researchers have discovered some reasons for these differences. Your culture and your life experience are partly responsible for your preferences for certain foods. Your food preferences are also partly genetic. (Your genetic preferences are the ones that you were born with.) In order to discover people's genetic preferences, researchers use a chemical called PROP. People taste it and respond to the taste. To some people, PROP has no flavor. The researchers classify these people as "nontasters." To other people, the flavor of PROP is a little bitter, or sharp. These people are "tasters." Then there are the people who can't stand the flavor of PROP. They find it to be unbearably bitter. These people are the "supertasters." Tasters have more taste buds on their tongues than nontasters do, and supertasters have many more taste buds than tasters do. This explains why supertasters are more sensitive to PROP and to the flavors in certain foods. So if you think the flavors in coffee, grapefruit juice, and broccoli are very strong, you may be a "supertaster."

Example: The topic of the reading passage is _____.
- (A) the flavor of coffee
- (B) becoming a supertaster
- (C) differences in people's taste sensitivity
- (D) research in the flavor of different foods

1. The main idea of the reading is that _____.
- (A) there are people who like different foods
- (B) there are cultural and genetic reasons for the differences in people's food preferences
- (C) some foods have a very strong flavor
- (D) PROPs can be used to identify different types of tastes

2. The meaning of *genetic* preferences is _____.
- (A) preferences for certain foods
- (B) preferences researchers have discovered
- (C) the preferences of some people
- (D) the preferences that people are born with

3. What is PROP?
- (A) a chemical
- (B) something that people are born with
- (C) a discovery
- (D) a researcher

4. Why do researchers use PROP?
   - (A) because it has no flavor
   - (B) to find out the responses to foods people were born with
   - (C) to discover the flavors in certain foods
   - (D) because people like its flavor

5. A food that is bitter has _____.
   - (A) no flavor
   - (B) little flavor
   - (C) a coffee flavor
   - (D) a sharp flavor

6. People who _____ are classified as *supertasters*.
   - (A) can't stand the flavor of PROP
   - (B) think that PROP has no flavor
   - (C) think that PROP tastes a little bitter
   - (D) like bitter flavors

7. Taste buds are probably _____.
   - (A) tiny pieces of food
   - (B) the small bumps on the surface of people's tongues
   - (C) chemicals in food that give it its flavor
   - (D) something in broccoli, grapefruit juice, and coffee

Reading Passage 2

A   After a cold, snowy winter, many people look forward to the long hot days of summer. The normal heat of summer can be pleasant. However, it's important to be aware that excessive—that is, too much—heat can be dangerous. There are other summer weather dangers, for example, tornadoes, lightning, and floods, but excessive heat kills more people each year than any of these. According to meteorologists (weather scientists), a heat wave is a period of excessive heat that lasts two days or more. A heat wave stresses people and can cause illnesses. These illnesses include heat cramps, heat exhaustion, and heat stroke. The people who are at the greatest risk during heat waves are the elderly, babies, and those with serious diseases.

B   High humidity (moisture in the air) can make the effects of heat even more harmful. As humidity increases, the air seems warmer than it actually is because it's more difficult for the body to cool itself through the evaporation of perspiration. During heat waves, meteorologists use the heat index to determine the level of danger. The heat index measures how hot it really feels when high humidity is added to the actual air temperature. As an example, if the air temperature is 95° F (Fahrenheit) and the humidity is 35%, the heat index is 98° F. But if the air temperature is 95° F and the humidity is 70%, the heat index is 124° F. Doctors say that even young, healthy people can die of heat stroke if they exercise outside when the heat index is high. During a heat wave, it's best to take it easy, drink plenty of water, and stay out of the heat as much as possible.

1. The main idea of Paragraph A is that _____.
   - (A) people look forward to the long hot days of summer
   - (B) too much heat can have dangerous effects
   - (C) tornadoes, lightning, and floods are dangerous
   - (D) meteorologists can define heat waves

2. The main idea of Paragraph B is that _____.
   - (A) humidity is moisture in the air
   - (B) meteorologists use the heat index during heat waves
   - (C) high humidity increases the danger of high air temperatures
   - (D) it's important to stay inside during a heat wave

3. The word *excessive* means _____.
   - (A) too much
   - (B) important
   - (C) long
   - (D) coming in waves

4. In the passage, lightning is mentioned as an example of _____.
   - (A) excessive heat
   - (B) a storm
   - (C) a stress on people
   - (D) a summer weather danger

5. A meteorologist is _____.
   - (A) a doctor
   - (B) a weather scientist
   - (C) a space scientist
   - (D) a dangerous weather condition

6. The heat index measures _____.
   - (A) the amount of moisture in the air
   - (B) air temperature
   - (C) a person's body temperature
   - (D) the temperature the body feels when heat and humidity are combined

7. Based on the information in the passage, which statement is true?
   - (A) Young, healthy people are more likely to die from excessive heat than elderly people are.
   - (B) The elderly, babies, and people with serious diseases are most likely to die from excessive heat, but it can kill young, healthy people, too.
   - (C) Perspiration is a dangerous effect of excessive heat.
   - (D) All heat waves include high humidity.

8. Why did the author write this passage?
   - (A) To warn people about the dangers of excessive heat and give suggestions about avoiding them.
   - (B) To give people useful information about the weather in the summer.
   - (C) To describe the work of meteorologists and their use of the heat index.
   - (D) To let people know how the body can cool itself naturally.

Reading Passage 3

A   Even though education is compulsory (required by law) for children in the United States, it is not compulsory for them to go to a conventional school to get that education. In every one of the 50 states, it is legal for parents to educate their children at home, or to "home school" their children. Although no state requires parents to have special training to home school their children, the regulations parents must follow vary widely from state to state. New Jersey, for example, imposes virtually no requirements. In contrast, New York requires home schoolers to notify their school districts, file instructional plans and frequent reports, and submit the results of tests or other forms of assessment for each child.

B   Increasing numbers of American families have been opting for home schooling. According to the National Center for Educational Statistics, about 1.1 million children were being home schooled in the spring of 2003. This represents an increase from the 850,000 who were being home schooled in the spring of 1999. In addition, the home-schooling rate—the percentage of the school-age population that was being home schooled—increased from 1.7 percent in 1999 to 2.2 percent in 2003.

C   A survey conducted in 2003 asked parents to give their most important reasons for home schooling their children. Thirty-one percent cited concerns about the environment in conventional schools, including safety, drugs, or negative peer pressure. Thirty percent said that the most important reason was to provide religious or moral instruction. Sixteen percent said that the most important reason was dissatisfaction with academic instruction at conventional schools. Parents gave other reasons, too; for instance, many said that they wanted to strengthen family bonds or allow their children more freedom.

D   It is difficult to show whether conventional schooling or home schooling works better. Home-schooled children tend to score significantly higher than the national average on college entrance tests. But educators say that it isn't easy to determine how meaningful the figures are, given the complexities of making direct comparisons. In the debate about home schooling, socialization is more of an issue than achievement. Advocates of conventional education believe that home-schooled children are at a disadvantage because they miss out on the kinds of social interaction and relationships with peers that are an essential part of a total education. Advocates of home schooling say that home-schooled children are not socially isolated; they think that home-schooled children have a larger social structure because they can be out in the world, in contact with people of different ages, and having experiences that they could never have in conventional schools.

Directions: For each question, choose the best answer based on the reading passage.

1. The word *conventional* means _____.
    - A relating to a meeting
    - B following what is normal or usual
    - C following a religion
    - D educational

2. According to the passage, increasing numbers of American families are choosing home schooling. What information does the author give to support this statement?
   - (A) In every one of the 50 states, it is legal for parents to educate their children at home.
   - (B) Thirty-one percent of parents say that the most important reason for home schooling is concerns about the environment in conventional schools.
   - (C) The number of children who were being home schooled increased from 850,000 in 1999 to about 1.1 million in 2003.
   - (D) A survey was conducted in 2003.

3. Scan (look quickly through) the passage to find the answer to this question: How many of the parents surveyed in 2003 said that the most important reason for home schooling their children was dissatisfaction with academic instruction at conventional schools?
   - (A) 1.1 million
   - (B) 30 percent
   - (C) 16 percent
   - (D) 2.2 percent

4. Three of the following statements give facts, and one gives an opinion. Based on the reading passage, which one is the opinion?
   - (A) Home-schooled children are at a disadvantage because they miss out on some kinds of social interaction and relationships.
   - (B) Thirty percent of parents who home school their children said that the most important reason was to provide religious or moral instruction.
   - (C) The home-schooling rate increased from 1.7 percent in 1999 to 2.2 percent in 2003.
   - (D) The regulations that parents of home schoolers must follow vary widely from state to state.

5. Which paragraph gives information about the number of home-schooled children who attend college?
   - (A) Paragraph B
   - (B) Paragraph C
   - (C) Paragraph D
   - (D) That information is not given in the passage.

6. In Paragraph D, the author implies, but does not state directly, that _____.
   - (A) home-schooled children tend to score significantly higher than the national average on college entrance tests
   - (B) it should be easy to make direct comparisons between conventional and home schooling
   - (C) parents are not academically qualified to teach their children
   - (D) there is controversy about the benefits of home schooling

7. Based on Paragraph D, we can conclude that advocates of conventional education object to home schooling mainly because home-schooled children _____.
   - (A) cannot achieve academically
   - (B) cannot be compared to conventionally educated children
   - (C) are not well socialized
   - (D) have too much freedom

Reading Passage 4

A   In recent years, the game of golf and golf tourism have grown in popularity in many places in the world. Golf, which traces its roots back to 15th century Scotland, is often viewed as a pleasant and harmless way to relax in a natural setting. But golf courses are not natural developments. They are artificial constructions that have a big environmental impact. As a result, there is often controversy about the building of golf courses.

B   Opponents of the use of land for golf courses bring up a number of environmental concerns. One is that a golf course covers a great deal of land, typically up to 200 acres, and in the process of developing this land into a golf course, it is common for fragile native ecosystems such as wetlands, rainforests, or coastal dunes to be destroyed. Indigenous grasses, shrubs, and trees are removed and replaced by foreign vegetation. The construction process causes soil erosion and results in the loss of biodiversity and habitat for wildlife. Another concern is the amount of chemical pesticides, herbicides, and fertilizers used to maintain the grass on a golf course once it is established. These chemicals can result in toxic contamination of the air, the soil, the surface water, and the underground water, and this in turn leads to health problems for people who live near the course or downstream from it, for people who work at the course, and even for the golfers. Yet another concern is that golf courses require an enormous amount of water every day. Their water consumption can lead to depletion of scarce fresh water resources. These and other concerns about golf courses have provoked protests, most recently in east and southeast Asia, against planned golf projects.

C   Designers, developers, and operators of golf courses have become increasingly aware of the environmental issues and of the protests. Consequently, they have sponsored research into more environmentally sensitive ways of constructing and maintaining courses. They believe that it is possible to build golf courses which protect and preserve the natural features of the landscape and natural habitats for wildlife. Their suggested practices include using native trees and shrubs, planting types of grass that require less water and are best adapted to the local climate, and using reclaimed water. Proponents of golf courses believe that these "green" golf courses can actually provide environmental benefits to their sites.

D   However, even a "green" golf course is likely to result in some environmental degradation and loss of habitat. Therefore, many biologists and wildlife ecologists, such as Lawrence Woolbright, a professor at Siena College in Albany, New York, contend that the best places to construct new golf courses are places that are already degraded, such as former landfills (garbage dumps) and old industrial sites, rather than on undeveloped land. A golf course that transforms a degraded site into a scenic landscape with wetlands and woodlands and habitat for wildlife could actually be a benefit to the environment.

1. Which of the following is the best statement of the main idea of the reading passage?
  - (A) Golf courses are artificial constructions, and are often built with no regard for the environment.
  - (B) Controversies about golf courses affect the tourist trade.
  - (C) Golf courses have significant effects on the environment, and these effects lead to controversy.
  - (D) Golf and golf tourism are growing in popularity internationally, leading to a more negative effect on the environment.

2. What word is opposite in meaning to the word *indigenous*? G B

    (A) native

    (B) foreign

    (C) natural

    (D) vegetation

3. Which of the following is *not* mentioned in the passage as a negative environmental impact of a golf course?

    (A) the destruction of fragile native ecosystems

    (B) soil erosion caused by cutting down trees

    (C) pollution caused by traffic and maintenance equipment

    (D) depletion of scarce fresh water resources

4. Which of the following best summarizes the environmental concerns of opponents of the use of land for golf courses?

    (A) They are concerned about the amount of land that a golf course covers.

    (B) They are concerned about the impact of the process of constructing new golf courses.

    (C) They are concerned about the impact of the maintenance of established golf courses.

    (D) All of the above.

5. Based on Paragraphs C and D, we can infer that a "green" golf course is one that _____.

    (A) consumes a great deal of water

    (B) is environmentally sensitive

    (C) is new and not degraded

    (D) has grass, shrubs, and trees

6. Based on the information in Paragraph C, we can conclude that _____.

    (A) it is certain that "green" golf courses have already been built

    (B) it is certain that "green" golf courses will be built in the future

    (C) it is not certain that any "green" golf courses have already been built or will be built in the future

    (D) opponents of golf courses accept the idea that "green" golf courses can actually provide environmental benefits to their sites

7. Based on Paragraph D, we can infer that the author of the passage _____.

    (A) agrees with Lawrence Woolbright

    (B) disagrees with Lawrence Woolbright

    (C) is willing to accept some environmental degradation and loss of habitat

    (D) is opposed to all golf courses

8. What would be an appropriate title for this reading passage?

    (A) A Brief History of Golf

    (B) Golf's Dirty Side

    (C) Why Make Golf Green?

    (D) The Beauty of Golf

Answer Key for Reading Strand Placement Test

Vocabulary I

1. A 2. B 3. D 4. C 5. B 6. A 7. D 8. D 9. B 10. A

Vocabulary II

1. C 2. B 3. B 4. D 5. B 6. A 7. D 8. C 9. D 10. D

Reading Passage 1

1. B 2. D 3. A 4. B 5. D 6. A 7. B

Reading Passage 2

1. B 2. C 3. A 4. D 5. B 6. D 7. B 8. B

Reading Passage 3

1. B 2. C 3. C 4. A 5. D 6. D 7. C

Reading Passage 4

1. C 2. B 3. C 4. D 5. B 6. C 7. A 8. C

SCORING FOR INTERACTIONS/MOSAIC READING PLACEMENT TEST	
Score	Placement
0–40	Interactions Access
41–55	Interactions 1
56–70	Interactions 2
71–85	Mosaic 1
86–100	Mosaic 2

This is a rough guide. Teachers should use their judgment in placing students and selecting texts.